ADJUST
THE VOLUME:

Find your frequency until the message is clear.

By Guylene Berry

For permission requests, write to the publisher, addressed "Attention: Permissions Coordinator," at the address below.

Amazon Publishing Center 420 Terry Ave N, Seattle, Washington, 98109, U.S.A

The opinions expressed by the Author are not necessarily those held by Amazon Publishing Center.

Ordering Information: Quantity sales and special discounts are available on quantity purchases by corporations, associations, and others. For details, contact the publisher at info@amazonpublishingcenter.com.

The information contained within this book is strictly for informational purposes. The material may include information, products, or services by third parties. As such, the Author and Publisher do not assume responsibility or liability for any third-party material or opinions. The publisher is not responsible for websites (or their content) that are not owned by the publisher. Readers are advised to do their own due diligence when it comes to making decisions.

Amazon Publishing Center works with authors and aspiring authors who have a story to tell and a brand to build. Do you have a book idea you would like us to consider publishing? Please visit AmazonPublishingCenter.com for more information.

Acknowledgements

God is so wonderful to me, and this book was born through His love, lessons, and ongoing guidance.

In addition to the Heavenly Father, I am forever grateful to every person who has been there for me and supported me throughout this journey. My mother and children have been my greatest inspiration and my driving forces every step of the way.

I'd also like to give my sisters a special shout-out because they have been in my corner for as long as I can remember. They have encouraged me and inspired me in ways that only sisters can. To every teacher who has helped me in my learning and shaped me into the person I am, I am forever grateful. I attract health, peace, freedom, transformation, growth, and abundance. All the challenges were there to help me grow into the person that I am today, and I am thankful for the opportunity to evolve.

Welcome

Adjust the Volume:
Find your frequency until the message is clear.

Is your vibration in alignment with what you're trying to manifest? In the future, your present moment will tell a story about how responsible you were for your past choices. Your thoughts and emotions shape your destiny. Position yourself for a mindset reset. You have the power to manage your emotions, pride, ego, and temptation, so be discerning about who and what you tolerate in your life. Own your story, and tune into the infinite power within you. Be intentional about your happiness and joy, protect your peace of mind, and practice gratitude.

Remain flexible, keep believing, forgive, create your path, and never lie to yourself. Know that the path is promising, and try not to dwell on the past. Remind ourselves that we are destined for greatness, which will motivate us to keep learning, evolving, and hoping. Our business is to keep working on our mindset, character, and intentions, so let us find and magnify our inner strength to bring out the deeper meaning in our lives.

Guylene Berry

As we only have limited time, it's important to focus on what's helpful and let go of the rest on our transformational journeys. By setting good intentions, we can achieve the best results.

The Koze Fanm show empowered me to use my voice and vision to make a positive impact. Each day presents a new opportunity to learn, grow, and level up, adjusting our volume and frequency to ensure our message is clear. We can uplift each other by sharing our knowledge and strength with those on similar paths. Through the show's music and daily topics, I felt a joyful connection with my audience and realized that gratitude can fortify us in our struggles. It's also an opportunity for us to grow, appreciate life, and achieve greatness by exercising our faith, positivity, and gratitude.

I've learned to trust the process and be thankful for the challenges that teach us valuable lessons. Getting to know ourselves, valuing our worth, and finding our purpose is important. Adjusting our volume and finding our frequency ensures our message is clear, and we all deserve to dream. Make the most of each day and follow your heart.

As a memoir, this book shares my experiences, wisdom, and knowledge acquired throughout my life. I offer it to you, dear reader, to connect with and be inspired by.

CONTENTS

PREFACE

I find myself in a state of transition after hosting the Koze Fanm syndicated show for nearly two decades. With this book, 'Adjust the Volume: Find Your Frequency Until the Message Is Clear,' I want to share my experiences inspired by my journey as a producer and host of the show. This book recounts how I took control of my feelings and emotions, focusing on providing hope and sharing positive energy with my audience. My passion for helping people finds its best expression through writing, allowing me to document my journey and inspire others as I continue to work towards fulfilling my purpose and mission. This endeavor has also heightened my awareness of my own vibration and overall well-being. My goal is to use my experiences as an opportunity to share my transformation and inspire others.

While this book covers my career in broadcasting and entrepreneurship, it also offers numerous valuable insights for aspiring entrepreneurs. As you delve into its pages, you'll find Reader Reflections, Journal Prompts, and tips to help you adjust your mindset and support you on your life journey.

I hope that by sharing the stories of my life, they serve as a reminder that it's time for you to step up. It's never too late to invest in your well-being, tap into your highest potential, and make your dreams come true. Sometimes, the path may be challenging before it becomes easy. However, you possess the power to reframe, re-energize, and refocus your thinking to activate your God-given potential.

What we should hold most dear in our lives are not material possessions but breakthrough moments that stay with us forever. Once we recognize the value of these moments and memories, we can begin to craft each moment with more intention and meaning. Our world reflects our mental state, so let's take action to move toward a Promised Land where we expect less and love more. Always remain aware of how to maintain your mental health and stability.

Contrary to music or talk shows on the radio, such as the Koze Fanm show, life has no replay or rewind. It is highly unpredictable, and each moment is fleeting. We possess the ability to shift the paradigm through the energy and frequency we emit. What we think, we attract. In my experience with the law of attraction, we can also refer to it as faith.

Though it may not always appear that way, remember that good intentions often yield positive results. We must live with purpose and be grateful for each moment. Always hold your head high and focus on welcoming positive energy because a positive attitude towards life can alter the outcome of most situations, especially in times of adversity. I particularly love the saying, 'La vie est belle' (Life is beautiful) because, regardless of life's outcomes, there's joy in recognizing that each new day presents an opportunity to begin anew, whether to triumph or to learn. Though I cannot predict the future, I am grateful for this time and space. The law of vibration, the law of attraction, and the law of cause and effect are three vital principles I've repeatedly encountered throughout my personal and professional journey.

At the outset of my talk show career, I returned to one of the radio stations where I had previously hosted. On that particular day, the board operator on duty decided it was time for me to start operating the control board myself. Without any prior training or guidance, I decided to give it a try. Despite feeling afraid, frustrated, and anxious, I managed to survive that day. However, controlling the board was just one of the many challenges I was facing at the time.

I needed to find sponsors, come up with daily topics for discussion, and learn to manage my time more efficiently, all while still working as a consultant. The radio show was an additional task on my already packed to-do list, and it was proving to be quite challenging.

The following day, I reached out to the late Junior Saint Surin to teach me how to manage and operate the board. Junior was the son of the owner of Radio Mega, one of the stations where I broadcasted the Koze Fanm show. He was incredibly willing to help me figure things out and advised me to pay close attention to how I adjusted the sound levels to ensure a well-balanced input and output. He assured me, 'I'm going to be there for you until you get it.'

Nearly two decades later, his words and actions continue to inspire me to spread hope through the airwaves with the Koze Fanm show. It's incredible to witness how even a little encouragement, kindness, and support can profoundly impact a person's life. Your words and actions can serve as a source of hope for others, whether through a small compliment or a smile. It's essential to remember that we all possess the power to make a positive difference in someone's day, even if it's just for a few hours each week, as I do on the Koze Fanm show.

Following his lesson, I've learned to keep adjusting the volume until the message is clear. This tip not only helped me get the sound right but also improved my connection with my audience. Life is a continuous process of adjusting the volume. With that in mind, how do we consistently realign our mindset to stay on course with this journey?

It's all about finding the perfect frequency when it comes to adjusting the volume while maintaining a clear message. Achieving balance in your physical and mental well-being, as well as your success and influence, can be attained through mindfulness practice. It's crucial to strategically allocate your time, energy, and finances to build reserves for life's challenges. Always remember that it's your responsibility to continually strive towards becoming the best version of yourself. Throughout the process of writing this book, I found inspiration from a Bible verse that deeply resonated with me.

James 1:19 (NIV). It says, "My dear brothers and sisters, take note of this: Everyone should be quick to listen, slow to speak, and slow to become angry."

I've overcome numerous challenges in my life, many of which I haven't discussed until now. The time has come to share it all. I'm allowing my story to become a resource to guide other women on their journeys, regardless of where they're headed. Now is the time to share a lifetime of experience as a mother, entrepreneur, woman in media, Haitian woman, and child of God.

It's as if all the challenging situations were just training, preparing us to soar higher into the light. So, let's live this life with joy inside us. These barriers and challenges don't disappear; they must be worked through. After investing so much time in overcoming the hurdles that life has thrown my way, I can now speak of my triumphs. I hope you can relate to these stories and discover how to adjust your mindset to reach the best version of yourself. Remember, your past does not determine your future.

If you take nothing else away from this, remember how crucial it is to start investing in yourself today. One day, you'll realize it was all part of the plan. Be strong and courageous. No matter how daunting it may seem, never stop believing in yourself. Understanding your weaknesses is as important as knowing your strengths. While humility is a virtue, it can be challenging to succeed in any meaningful endeavor without confidence in yourself and your potential.

The simple rule of success in life is to think and play like a champion and watch how you evolve. There's always a price to pay, but is it worth it? Be aware that increasing your well-being requires daily, intentional effort over extended periods. Knowledge is also a great confidence booster; goals become more achievable when broken down into manageable steps. Equally important is the need to 'unlearn' things that have boxed us in and hindered our growth. Personally, I had to unlearn the belief that 'therapy is for crazy people.' In my opinion, therapy is for those seeking solutions to their issues, gaining clarity, and it can work wonders."

Personal growth is an ongoing journey that never truly ends. As we evolve, we become increasingly aware of the areas where we can improve. It's crucial to remain authentic so that God can work through us. Always stay true to yourself, be honest, and embrace your uniqueness. Challenges have much to teach us, and it's important to understand that failure is a natural part of the path to success. Facing obstacles head-on, seeking assistance, and asking for God's help, for He is always by our side, are recommended approaches.

I hope that my story will serve as an inspiration on your own journey. Instead of dwelling in self-pity, use your challenges as stepping stones toward success. Remember that you possess greater strength than you may realize; be confident and unstoppable. This is the key to thriving under pressure. Believe in your dreams and tirelessly work towards their fulfillment. Despite any setbacks, I remain optimistic about the future because of the choices I make today.

Progress is a journey, not a destination. Embrace every opportunity to learn and grow, and commit to being a lifelong learner. It's in this commitment that you'll discover power, knowledge, experience, and true liberation.

CHAPTER ONE
Allow Me to
Reintroduce Myself

I am Guylene Berry, the founder of Koze Fanm Network and Alliance for Progress, Inc. I am a black immigrant Haitian woman. Being who I am and knowing that God loves me is a lifelong privilege. I am known as someone with a wide range of interests; however, my main one is to be a source of inspiration. In 2006, I founded the Koze Fanm Network to serve as a platform for using my voice to inspire and empower others, as my mission is to be the change I want to see in my community. I believe that women's issues are everyone's issues. I used the radio to share resources and information to empower others, helping them discover lasting solutions to improve their lives. At the beginning of my journey as an entrepreneur, I worked as a Haitian Creole freelance interpreter, all while being a single mother, which was incredibly challenging. I started with little resources, filled with fear and feeling unprepared. But as I continue to work on this canvas, I've come to realize that there is always time to change and start again, reset, re-strategize, or re-adjust; life is a series of adaptations. It's been a unique and exciting journey, and it continues. I want to invite you to join me on this journey.

My mission is to be the best version of myself and utilize my experience and knowledge to provide people with the tools to live a better life, recognizing that I am continually learning myself. We live in a time when endless information is available for us to access, and it's also an opportunity to rethink how we perceive media and evolve as individuals. It's important to understand that life doesn't have to be perfect to be excellent; we should focus on living in the present moment and inspiring others to achieve their goals. I am committed to taking the necessary steps to let go of old memories that no longer serve me and transform my mind to gain the clarity I need to fulfill my God-given purpose. I am determined to be my authentic self, knowing that controlling my emotions while helping others find their own light and purpose is essential. I am in the process of creating the best version of myself, and though it may take time, the goal is to be proud of my progress today, understanding that what lies ahead is better than what's behind. I am grateful for the beauty that surrounds me, and I am committed to stepping away from unnecessary drama to preserve my peace. I appreciate the lessons from my past and eagerly anticipate a brighter future while embracing who I am today and allowing God to be my guiding compass.

My name is Guylene, and I was born in Haiti in the 1970s. I am the youngest among my mother's children. I believe that everyone should have access to basic necessities, including good health, safety, education, freedom, prosperity, and a sense of belonging. Coming from Haiti, I see that there are many unmet needs, and I am constantly seeking ways to better serve and contribute. As I learn to make room for more blessings in my life, forgiving both myself and others and delving deeper into self-discovery, I consider it my most significant ongoing project. This journey represents my continuous evolution and growth. To me, personal growth is an everlasting process, but it has also been one of the most rewarding experiences that has allowed me to understand the grand plans that God has in store for me. I've come to realize that we have the power to overcome our fears and that with unwavering faith, anything is possible.

Isaiah 43:1

But now, this is what the Lord says, He who created you, Jacob, He who formed you, Israel: 'Do not fear, for I have redeemed you; I have summoned you by name; you are mine."

I can relate to a time in my life when I used to worry incessantly and seek to understand everything. It was an exhausting period. Life is indeed filled with uncertainty, and we often find ourselves preoccupied with the future or the unknown. While many things remain beyond our control, our mindset plays a crucial role in how we handle challenging circumstances. With confidence, we can face the unknown because, with God by our side, we know that we are more than conquerors.

The Bible says, "We are hard-pressed on every side, but not crushed; perplexed, but not in despair; persecuted, but not abandoned; struck down, but not destroyed."
(2 Corinthians 4:8-9 NIV)

As I strive to find my frequency, adjust my volume, and cultivate self-awareness, I am also focused on striking the right balance between my heart and my mind. My journey is not about competing with others or winning a trophy; it's about becoming a better version of myself and serving others more effectively. My aim is to discover meaning and fully embrace the person God created me to be. I encourage you to embark on a similar journey because our attitude amidst life's challenges is often more significant than the circumstances themselves.

When I reflect on my life, I realize that I still have a long way to go. However, when I look back at where I used to be, I am filled with gratitude for all the progress I've made.

Professional Background

In life, it's essential not to remain stagnant; we must continually reinvent ourselves and strive for new heights. It takes courage to reach for those new heights while also getting to know who we truly are and pursuing the purpose that God has bestowed upon us. It's crucial to understand that we cannot give what we don't possess, including self-love, self-forgiveness, and self-satisfaction. We are inherently deserving of good health, joy, wealth, and dignity. On the journey to manifesting your reality, it's important to tap into your intuition. One valuable lesson I've learned about life is that sometimes the strongest-looking individuals around us are silently enduring pain, shedding tears behind closed doors, and battling personal demons that no one else is aware of, all while hoping for a positive change in their circumstances. Sometimes, in order to build something new, we must take action, and for me, prayer has been the most powerful tool. God has promised us that we are not alone in our struggles, and He is with us always.

Jashua 1:5 No one will be able to stand against you all the days of your life. As I was with Moses, so I will be with you; I will never leave you nor forsake you.

Living in South Florida, I witness the constant rise of new buildings and construction projects every day. We can draw a valuable parallel from this by applying the same idea or blueprint to improve our lives. Just as we build a solid foundation for a structure through knowledge and self-awareness, we must do the same for ourselves. Regardless of the path one chooses in life, the pursuit of personal development is essential for reaching our highest level of self-awareness and self-actualization, ultimately paving the way for the pursuit of excellence. I want to emphasize that while things may not always go as planned, we possess the power to make necessary adjustments. Let's don our creative hats, filter and refine our thoughts, and recognize that we all have the opportunity to transform our lives. It begins with being present and seizing the moment, facing life's challenges with grace and joy, and finding contentment in the here and now. Reflecting on my high school experience, I recall signing up for a media class where I learned the basics of broadcasting, skills that I continue to use on my shows today. At the time, my intention was merely to fill my schedule with an easy class, and I had yet to discover my true calling in life. Although the idea of hosting and producing my own radio or TV show seemed appealing at the time, it wasn't a passion I expected to pursue immediately, if at all. However, it's important to remember that patience is a virtue in life. Regularly evaluate yourself, understanding that change takes time, and be sure to celebrate your victories along the way. From a vague idea to nearly two decades of making a difference on the airwaves, my journey serves as a testament to the power of perseverance and the value of self-discovery.

As life continued to unfold, I got married at the age of 21, relocated from Haiti to New Jersey, and began my journey of raising children. A few years later, I made another move, this time from New Jersey to North Miami, where I briefly worked for my mom, assisting her in sending goods to Haiti for her import-export business. Subsequently, my career path led me through various work experiences, but one role stood out as my favorite – that of an interpreter. This profession provided me with invaluable insights into people and the judicial system. The experience also played a significant role in shaping my career in radio.

One of the fundamental communication lessons I acquired from my time as an interpreter was the importance of being an active listener. This skill was crucial in legal settings and required a deep sense of empathy and an understanding of the diverse parties involved. It enabled me to serve as a bridge, overcoming the barriers of language and culture. Growing up in Haiti and frequently traveling to the United States from a young age equipped me with fluency in both English and Haitian Creole, along with a profound understanding of both cultures.

In 1998, I embarked on my journey as a medical interpreter, specializing in assisting Haitian individuals living in Miami. I worked for a company that had a contract with workers' compensation aimed at aiding injured employees in their therapy sessions. My role was to facilitate communication, bridging the language gap, and ensuring that these injured workers understood their prognosis and could fully benefit from their therapy sessions.

Shortly after stepping into the role of a medical interpreter, a friend of mine, Dr. Claudia Bonilla, introduced me to a valuable resource for obtaining my certification as a court interpreter. Before long, I successfully earned my certification through Berlitz, a renowned language education and leadership training program. This opened up opportunities for me to become actively involved in immigration interpretation services. Over time, I transitioned into working with mediation courts and family courts. Initially, I operated as a freelancer, but later, I served as a state employee at the Broward County Courthouse.

Each case I interpreted in the courts allowed me to connect with individuals facing various hardships. After years of working in this field, I realized that while numerous resources existed to assist people in different situations, the Haitian Community often had limited access to such resources. However, as a state employee, I encountered certain restrictions in freely sharing information despite my strong desire to support my community.

For instance, I witnessed numerous instances where parents of minors had to witness their children being sent to juvenile detention for periods exceeding 21 days, often for minor offenses or misdemeanors. What

many of them didn't know was that their children could have complet-
ed educational programs instead of serving time in detention.

Similarly, I encountered cases involving individuals with mental health
issues who found themselves facing criminal charges they might not
have committed if their mental health struggles had been adequately
addressed or treated. These individuals were unaware that acknowledging their mental health issues and using them as a defense could
have provided them with the help they needed as an alternative
to incarceration.

In numerous custody cases, disputes often revolved around money,
with many parties failing to recognize that quality time spent with their
children is a crucial aspect of nurturing well-adjusted kids. Child support goes beyond being a mere financial transaction.

These are just a few of the lessons I've gleaned from my experiences,
and it was particularly challenging not being able to share this valuable insight with others to assist them. This experience ignited a spark
within me, leading me to make it my mission to find ways to support
the Haitian community in South Florida, helping them access these essential resources. This initiative opened the door to countless opportunities for me.

As I transitioned into my role as the official Haitian Creole interpreter
for the City of Miami and took on the position of a promotion assistant in the communication department, I continued my commitment
to serving this underserved community. I provided interpretation services at committee board meetings and community events, which further exposed me to an array of resources and programs available to
benefit the community.

My experience as a Creole court interpreter provided me with clarity of
purpose and helped me find my rhythm. One day, while I was working
at the Broward County court, I was selected as a Creole interpreter to
accompany the court-appointed psychiatrist to the jail for the examination of a Haitian man. I would refer to this experience as 'a taste of
freedom.' As I was identified and proceeded to meet with the doctor

and the inmate for his psychological evaluation, a loud bang echoed behind me. The heavy metal doors in the jail had a way of making one feel uncomfortable. Despite my initial eagerness to complete this assignment, as it meant I could go home early, the jarring sound of that gate haunted me for days.

Jumping into the Radio Business

I aspired to become the woman of my dreams. To achieve this, I had to confront my fears, undergo a personal reinvention, and reset my mindset. Taking charge of the life I desired became my primary focus. It was in the year 2006 that I fully embraced this mission, drawing upon my years of experience, and I discovered my calling to serve the community more effectively. I found solace in the belief that I can overcome all challenges through Christ, and I am never alone. Though it might not be easy, it is undeniably possible.

I distinctly recall reaching out to numerous radio presenters, requesting them to share valuable information with their listeners. However, this was separate from their willingness to include a live-read Public Service Announcements (PSAs) segment during their paid airtime. Determined to disseminate essential information and resources within the Haitian community in South Florida, I took it upon myself to step into this role. The desire to share meaningful insights persisted.

During a conversation with Ed Lozama, a renowned radio talk show host in Haiti and South Florida, I expressed my interest in launching my own show. I had an abundance of ideas that I wished to share with the community. Ed Lozama not only encouraged me at the outset of my journey in hosting my own show but also assisted me in choosing the name "Koze Fanm," which translates to "Women's Issues" in Creole."

The transition from being a full-time employee as a court interpreter to becoming an entrepreneur and radio show host was not as smooth as I had anticipated. Despite having a background in media and communications training, I realized that I still had much to learn. For me, the journey of effective communication is an ongoing process. Additionally, as a woman, I faced the added challenge of entering a predominantly male-dominated industry. In the beginning, I didn't feel particularly welcome. It was as if there was no seat at the table for me, so I took it upon myself to create one and extend invitations to others.

I managed to secure some weekend airtime, which is often considered a coveted slot in the radio industry. The important thing was that I had taken the first step. Nevertheless, I had to allocate funds to pay the station for my time slot.. My debut on-air happened one Sunday afternoon on March 5, 2006. As the operator switched on my microphone, I found myself frozen in nervousness.

"Just say something, anything, to the listeners," he encouraged me.

Fortunately, I had one of my favorite literary works with me, and I began with a quote that would set the tone for all my future broadcasts. The opening words of my show were a Bible verse:

"But those that wait upon the LORD shall renew their strength; they shall mount up with wings as eagles; they shall run, and not be weary, and they shall walk, and not faint." (Isaiah 40:31 NIV)

That set the tone for the rest of my career. Nearly two decades later, I still play a gospel song whenever I'm on the air and share the quote of the day. Without God as my guiding force, I wouldn't be where I am today. He is all-powerful and all-knowing, my source of strength and salvation. The days of misery are over when you reach the point of trusting in God. By sharing the gospel on the air, I can help others build a trusting relationship with God and cultivate hope.

Another significant challenge was that I had to pay for airtime entirely out of my pocket since, at the time, I still needed sponsors, at least for the first three months. I was compelled to take swift action to make it all happen. I took on two part-time jobs to support myself and my children during this transition. These two jobs aligned perfectly with the purpose of my consulting journey; I aspired to become a community engagement specialist.

13

One of these jobs brought me back to the City of Miami, where I worked as the Promotional Assistant to Kelly Penton, the former Communications Director of Miami. Kelly recognized my passion for serving others, opened the door for me, and offered me this paid position. As the Promotional Assistant, my role involved genuine community engagement. Additionally, I had the opportunity to contribute to and host the local TV show, "Bonjou Miami," on Channel 77 for a couple of years. The show was broadcast on the official channel of the City of Miami.

During that time, I also gained valuable experience in communications by doing voice-overs, creating Creole commercials, and providing translations for the State Emergency Operations Center of the City of Miami. I even hosted local segments to discuss city improvements and hurricane preparedness on "Bonjou Miami" on channel 77.

Grow, Expand, and Never Stop Learning

To improve is to change, live your best, and think your best each day. Do what you love often, and remember to keep your life simple. We all have the right to be prosperous, healthy, loved, fulfilled, and happy. What are you doing today to bring yourself closer to your dreams? Who are you, and what defines you? What are your intentions? I have asked myself these questions many times throughout my life. The answers serve me well every time, giving me the courage to keep moving forward. With consistency and good intentions, ordinary people can achieve extraordinary things. Growth is never easy, but it is essential. At this point in my career, I also had another consulting job with the Community Redevelopment Agency (CRA) of North Miami. This opportunity provided me with an inside look at how government functions in terms of development, infrastructure, mixed-use projects, affordable housing, and beautification. While the organization wanted to hire me full-time, I chose to remain in my communication job with the City of Miami as a Promotional Assistant in the communication department. Although I could have taken on both full-time and part-time roles, doing so would have placed significant constraints on my time and hindered my ability to give my best effort to all the projects I was involved in while also fulfilling my responsibilities as a single mother and entrepreneur. Being a single mother in business can be challenging, but it's also a fantastic experience and an opportunity to be creative and involve my children in some of the activities. The perspectives of young people can be a valuable asset in the process.

I was incredibly dedicated to the hustle, but my commitment to integrity and values was even stronger. I later realized that self-preservation is paramount for maintaining one's sanity and well-being. Just because an opportunity comes knocking doesn't mean you have to immediately embrace it. Take the time to evaluate and double-check. Many more opportunities will come your way, and some may appear suitable, but trust me, it's essential to deliberate on which opportunities you choose.

Working hard is a necessity, but it's equally important to be selective with your commitments. My mom, Talina, used to advise me to 'work hard while learning how to work smart.'

During this time, I also started shadowing Rodney Baltimore from Hot 105 FM to gain more technical experience in radio broadcasting. He was my mentor in the early years and taught me everything from sound levels, inputs, and outputs to keeping an audience engaged. I had the privilege of being a guest on several segments of Rodney's show, including one about the 2010 earthquake in Haiti and announcements of community events.

One of the most valuable lessons I learned from him was the significance of being fully present and tuned in to the show rather than letting my mind wander elsewhere. To deliver an excellent show, I had to stop allowing external circumstances to disrupt my focus and inner peace. The lesson is to control what you can manage and govern your emotions. Your mindset's inputs and outputs shape the outcome of your desired life. If I couldn't prevent something, I had to refuse to let it create stress and find ways to refocus, reset, and re-strategize. Rejection is an opportunity to readjust; our responsibility is to maintain a positive mindset even when circumstances may appear bleak.

Within a little while of launching the show, I got into a better rhythm. I became more comfortable on-air, and I began hosting shows on two more radio stations: one in Boston, California, and another in Atlanta, through the network of Chenet Nerette. I also hosted shows in Orlando on Radio Panik and here in South Florida on WSRF (1580 AM), Radio Mega (1700 AM), and WLQY (1320 AM). This meant I had seven hours of weekly airtime from Monday through Saturday.

For many years, I stayed up late and woke up early to optimize my time and successfully juggle all the roles I had taken on for myself and my family. Balancing work with my responsibilities as a single mother while also being an active member of the community was challenging at times. It pushed me to my limits and showed me what I was capable of.

To this day, I have to keep reminding myself that the goal is not perfection; it's progression. I've come to understand that if I want more consistency in my life, I have to work to create it. I've realized that I am the product of my decisions and choices, not of my circumstances, even when we sometimes have to make the best of a lousy decision. There were many times when I felt like giving up on the show because I faced so much resistance and encountered many roadblocks. Sometimes, I wondered if it was necessary. Dealing with my personal issues made the challenges seem even more intense. In retrospect, I'm glad I never gave up because I have come so far, and God helped me through every moment. The love, the light, and the lessons are priceless.

I went from hosting one hour each Sunday afternoon to creating a syndicated radio and TV show and doing so much more in the community. I founded a not-for-profit organization to empower and provide opportunities for youth to learn about broadcasting and public speaking firsthand. These experiences allowed me to share my truth in Koze Fanm magazines, syndicated radio, an international TV show, and now a book. When I look back, the journey was terrifying at times but incredibly gratifying.

The show was designed to address vital topics to help and contribute to the Haitian community's growth and progress. Key topics include education, health and wellness, finance, legal issues, culture, relationships, parenting, and social issues affecting Black Lives, Caribbean communities, and immigrants. Our mission is "Providing Hope through the Airwaves."

One day, an older lady who listened to the show approached me and said, "Don't give up, my darling. I'm proud of what you're doing on the show; you're very talented. Keep going because the work you are doing now will transform many generations and always brings me joy when the show comes on the air." What she said ignited something in me and instilled deep-seated courage and determination to move forward.

I went beyond hosting the Koze Fanm show and pursued various training, certifications, and licenses to help and empower others. In addition to our life experiences, being equipped and prepared for growth is essential. We must learn to train our minds to be stronger than our feelings. Often, when we think we are at the end of something, we are actually at the beginning of something else, something more fulfilling. On our journey to our destiny, there will be twists and turns—always remember that God has your back.

As I gain a deeper understanding of my purpose and calling, I increasingly believe that with God on my side, all things are possible. When you prioritize God and do your part, it becomes an opportunity to live your passion with deeper meaning. God is almighty and promises to support us. Have faith and know that the possibilities are endless. Let's stop playing small and get to work!

To me, consistent progress is a success, regardless of how slow it may seem, as long as we don't stop. And don't forget to smile along the way.

In this process, I've learned that if you're going to pursue something, go all in. Even if fear holds you back initially, your courage will eventually prevail. The journey will be unique for each person, but challenge yourself to confront the things that scare you the most. Though it may sound a bit cliché, some of the best things in life are found outside of our comfort zones.

Discovering your limits and pushing them to a point that opens the right doors is crucial. Realize that nobody else possesses your voice, vision, or experiences. Sometimes, we must have the confidence to move forward and seek places where our talents are both valued and appreciated. Keep investing in yourself to enhance your ability to manage different opportunities. You may not always achieve your initial objective, but the experiences gained are truly priceless. Write your life story and use it as a foundation to become your own hero, strive for personal growth, and leave a lasting legacy.

Opening Doors for Others Along the Way

I appreciate everything that people have done for me to bring me to where I am today. We are all interconnected, and each of us has a role to play in making the world a better place, both in the present moment and for the next generation. Know that we don't have to be perfect to make a positive impact. While discovering a new passion in life, I've realized that helping others find their purpose is dear to me, utilizing my knowledge and experience. My objective is to become more of a team player, a collaborator, and an advocate. I need to continue working on myself to feel more confident in delivering the message with ease and establishing better connections. As I continue to engage in conversations about empowering the Caribbean and Haitian communities in South Florida, I understand that the things we learn along the way should be put into service to assist and empower others in finding their own path. I aimed to break down barriers that created unnecessary challenges for both myself and others, so I shared the knowledge I gained during my many years as an interpreter for the courts and various municipalities throughout South Florida.

Here are some tips for living a more enriched life: Accept that we all have limitations and challenges. Sometimes, the person whose life seems the easiest has faced the greatest difficulties; they have struggles but respond differently. Don't dwell on the past. Dream, believe, stay busy, and enjoy the process. Stop waiting for approval and validation from others to start pursuing your God-given purpose. Be patient and make space for your blessings.

Mental health and wellness have been central topics on my show since well before the onset of COVID-19. Within Haitian and other Caribbean cultures, there has been a pervasive negative stigma surrounding mental health issues, which has served as the root cause of many other problems within our community. The refusal to acknowledge and address these issues, especially among men, has resulted in numerous unfavorable situations and cycles that could have been prevented if mental health concerns were openly discussed on a regular basis through my show.

I have made it a priority to break down this stigma and have consistently invited mental health specialist Dr. Vardy Pharel to appear on my show, providing scientifically backed resources to those who need them most. My show also seamlessly integrates discussions on faith and spirituality, recognizing that mental and physical wellness requires a multi-faceted approach.

In the ensuing years, numerous opportunities have arisen that align closely with my mission and passion. I have had the privilege of training over 50 young individuals, including both of my children, in the fields of radio broadcasting and entrepreneurship. This initiative was sponsored by my nonprofit organization, the Alliance for Progress (formerly known as the "Positive Impact Foundation"). Our project, known as the Youth Talk Show, aimed to help local teenagers develop essential public speaking skills and foster connections with their peers, particularly in relation to the shared experiences of being the children of immigrants.

Additionally, I undertook another side project called "Vwa Diaspora," which translates to "Diaspora's Voice." This radio show airs every Saturday following the Youth Talk Show and addresses the various challenges encountered by the Haitian diaspora while also exploring ideas for building a more sustainable foundation for Haiti. "Vwa Diaspora" is a call-in show designed to galvanize the community into action and inspire positive change in Haiti.

In 2009, another fantastic opportunity presented itself that would open many doors for me in the future. State Representative Yolly Roberson recommended me to the Governor's office, Charlie Crist, for appointment as a member of the State Count Committee for the 2010 Census. My role was to represent the Caribbean Community in various meetings with the specific aim of helping the government better understand the needs of the Haitian Caribbean-American community.

The experience I gained as a part of the State Count Committee made me realize that my radio shows were a good starting point, but the information I shared needed to reach a broader audience. In 2011, I re-evaluated my role as merely a radio show host and founded a media agency called Sak Pase Media with the goal of making a more significant impact. The purpose of this agency was to secure sponsorships from various governmental agencies, organizations, and businesses seeking to connect with the Haitian community and serve as a bridge.

The birth of Sak Pase Media rekindled an entrepreneurial spirit that had long lived within me. It provided me with a platform to offer practical solutions, facilitate financial exchanges, bring more resources and opportunities to the community, and enable more people to access opportunities that could transform their lives.

A Unique Skill Set

Not all of us possess equal talents; however, we can develop our skills and knowledge through training, education, and the experiences of others. Developing the ability to radiate positive energy, be friendly, and remain genuine has opened many doors for me to connect with people. It's always beneficial to bring your own light and maintain an optimistic outlook. I firmly believe that the right attitude will attract the right people into my life. Be open to sharing your positive vibes with others. Growing up in Haiti and having the opportunity to travel to New York when I was five years old provided me with a unique perspective on how I perceive and interact with others. It gave me the exposure and experience needed to become proficient in both languages and to understand both cultures. This early exposure allowed me to serve as a bridge between Haitians and other ethnic groups.

Values make all the difference, so I began to prioritize and value my time in order to bring about a shift in my life. This transformation didn't happen overnight. However, today, I am trained and experienced in several areas:

Radio/TV broadcaster

- Producer
- Professional and personal development trainer
- Business Consultant
- Human Rights consultant
- Community outreach strategist
- Life/ relationship coach
- Image consultant
- Licensed life and health insurance broker
- Licensed real estate agent
- Painting Contractor construction trade.
- Entrepreneur
- Chaplain
- And more

You possess the ability to achieve greatness, irrespective of your identity or origin. I am a mother, entrepreneur, and community advocate with a wealth of experience that has imparted valuable lessons to me. I have no regrets; my faith in God, the experiences, the victories, and the lessons have shaped me into the person I am today. However, I now recognize that I could have been kinder to myself in my younger years.

Progress commences with acknowledging the need for change and understanding that reinventing oneself is crucial. Asking questions is essential for self-awareness and personal growth. When I pose questions to myself, I become more aware of specific issues and confidently seek answers and improvements.

God has been my guiding force throughout my journey, and I acknowledge that He is the source of my supply. He has empowered me to use my voice and knowledge to help others lead a more purposeful life. In 2006, I realized that waiting for someone to provide me with a platform to share my message with my community was not sufficient. So,

I summoned the courage to answer my calling, which was a significant step forward. Although finding my authentic voice and message took time and effort, I am confident in the positive impact I am making through my syndicated show, Koze Fanm, and Sak Pase Media. Being a court interpreter was good, but now I am truly making a difference in people's lives.

When taking charge of your journey, there are three key things to always keep in mind:

1. Be mindful of the way you are using your words because   you can never take them back after they are out.
2. Your thoughts, because you have to protect your peace at all costs (most battles are won in mind, not on the field)
3. Be aware that we are fighting battles that no one is aware of.
4. Clear out the old energy to welcome new ones.
5. Be mindful of your time and how you use it.

Hosting the Koze Fanm radio show is a very serious matter to me. Being a woman in the predominantly male-dominated media world at the time, I vividly remember feeling insecure and uncertain about my future in the broadcasting business when I began in 2006.

In hindsight, the entire experience has opened my eyes, although I couldn't fully grasp the significance of the journey back then. Starting the show from scratch and with little experience, I am immensely grateful to have come this far. It was only possible because I persevered in the face of adversity, even though I contemplated quitting many times.

I now realize that, just as I was learning how to do the radio show, I was also discovering who I was and what I wanted to become. Throughout my years of hosting the Koze Fanm show, I faced numerous challenges, including divorce, single motherhood, foreclosure, bankruptcy, the loss of my mother, nearly losing my business, and much more.

Despite these immense challenges in my life, I always found clarity by reminding myself to refocus and "adjust the volume." Knowing that the joy of the Lord is my strength holds profound meaning for me.

Reader Reflection

"Do not be anxious about anything, but in every situation, by prayer and petition, with thanksgiving, present your requests to God. And the peace of God, which transcends all understanding, will guard your hearts and your minds in Christ Jesus." - Philippians 4:6-7 (NIV)

"All hard work brings a profit, but mere talk leads only to poverty."
- Proverbs 14:23 (NIV)

"Do not conform to the pattern of this world, but be transformed by the renewing of your mind. Then you will be able to test and approve what God's will is—his good, pleasing and perfect will." - Romans 12:2 (NIV)

Journal Prompts

Before we go any further, ask yourself a couple of questions to check where you are in life and what your purpose is so that you can move intentionally as you are navigating through life.

1. How do you see yourself?
2. Is there a decision that you are struggling to make?
3. What do you want to get out of life?
4. What are you currently trying to achieve?
5. What are you working on today to prepare for your future?

Tips to Adjust the Volume

- Reflect on what you want to see happening in your life.
- Use your failures and turn them into lessons.
- Start reading and be open to learning more.
- Get out of toxic situations to protect your peace of mind.
- Stay committed to your goal. It's okay to change the plan but not the goal.

CHAPTER TWO
Putting the Pieces Together

What vision do you have for yourself? Set your mind to find the freedom to pursue your dream. Take time to get to know yourself and examine your actions, make a declaration of faith, and watch your dreams come true. The concept of 'Adjust the Volume' is about resetting your mind and recognizing that you have the ability to become a better version of yourself, allowing God to take you to the next level. These three things are essential for your self-improvement journey, and a growth mindset entails dreaming, believing, and achieving. God works in mysterious ways, and faith doesn't necessarily make things easy, but it makes them possible. He can use any difficulty and turn it around to fulfill His purpose through us. Stay calm when facing challenges or rejections, understanding that these are signs of redirections. As stated in Genesis 50:20, 'You intended to harm me, but God intended it for good to accomplish what is now being done, the saving of many lives.'

The best way to overcome a poverty mindset is to acquire skills that will help you be more mindful of what you read, listen to, and watch. Reposition yourself and explore new ways of thinking. Choose wisely because every situation is an opportunity to learn something new, grow, and find solutions that can benefit you and others. We all experience defining moments. In 2012, I made the decision not to settle and started to think my way out of a very difficult situation. Sometimes, a fall can mark the beginning of something great. Allow the light to shine in, and don't dwell on the past. Keep building, and never cease in your search for what makes your soul smile. Stay unattached to the outcome.

Since 2010, my life has changed in a variety of ways, a series of events began to unfold, ultimately leading to where I am today from the earthquake that hit Haiti on January 12, 2010. One vivid memory stands out from June 2018: as I was returning from Jacmel, Haiti, en route to Port-au-Prince to catch my flight back to the United States and visit my mother, I found myself stranded on the road in Gressier for over eight hours, despite it being just an hour's drive to Port-au-Prince. This unexpected delay was due to a protest, causing me to miss my flight to Miami that day.

During those seemingly endless eight hours, which should have taken only two and a half hours from Jacmel, I was unable to step out of the vehicle to stretch, grab a meal, or use the restroom. It was during this time, confined on the bus, that I was compelled to contemplate a better way to enhance my life, position myself for success, continue being a blessing to others, and focus on reaching the next level. This incident marked a defining moment when I pondered whether I should remain in the United States or return to Haiti. I came to realize that there exists a certain level of consciousness and understanding to attain. I firmly told myself that my foremost priority should be my mental health and overall well-being. Regardless of the number of degrees one may have achieved, a negative mindset will never yield positive life outcomes. What are your core values and principles, and how will you actualize them in your present and future self?

The motivation to reorganize your life and persevere during challenging times lies within you. If you often find yourself thinking, "Why didn't I do things differently?" well, that's a promising start. You stand on the precipice of a new beginning with the opportunity to make positive changes. Keep your focus on your goals because you possess the ability to make different choices now while you still can. Self-improvement is an ongoing journey toward greatness. Both personal and professional growth involves continuously upgrading yourself and maintaining a clear vision for your life. Feel free to make adjustments along the way.

Reprogramming Yourself: It's crucial to first acknowledge your current state and re-strategize before redirecting your focus toward something new in your life. Refuse to let any negative influences take root in your life. Release your doubts and proceed with unwavering faith. Understand that you possess the power to bring about positive change. The question you should ask is, "What needs to be changed?"

Seek knowledge and understanding actively. Consider enrolling in new classes, whether in person or online, delve into books, and seek mentorship. Cultivate new habits that will enhance your life, such as exploring new places and nurturing your creativity. Life is an ongoing journey of learning, and even if the education isn't formally accredited, it can still be incredibly inspiring. Investing in your education yields a valuable return because knowledge is something that can never be taken from you; it only increases your worth and value.

Among the most precious gifts I've given myself are those of self-development, self-interest, and transformation. Let me share a question I've posed to myself on numerous occasions: "What kind of person do I aspire to become?" This seemingly simple question has motivated me to continually acquire new skills and evolve into the best version of myself. Keep moving forward, no matter how many setbacks you may encounter.

Looking back, I've realized that what I did to survive will not enable me to thrive. In shaping your tomorrow, create what's true to you. We are not conjuring something from nothing; we must take what we have and make it better. As children of God, we all possess greatness within us.

What is Success?

Become more open-minded and mindful, recognizing that frustrations are an integral part of the process, it's not always easy. Put a smile on your face. You are already on the right path to success because you acknowledge your uniqueness and believe in hard work, dedication, good intentions, and prayer. Strive to do your best, engage in activities that fill you with pride, have a meaningful purpose, set ambitious goals while also seeking stability, and steer clear of negative self-talk. Always remember that you are intelligent, worthy, loved, beautiful, and more than enough. We don't need to have all the answers, but we must dedicate time to self-reflection and continuous growth. Let's not become fixated on our agendas; instead, let's cultivate the skills of flexibility and adaptability, which are crucial for our ongoing development. We learned this lesson in 2020 when we had to adapt to the new normal of COVID-19. It was a stark reality check, requiring us to focus on self-care, physical and mental health, and adapting to distance learning. During this time, we yearned for more of life's simple pleasures and had to become comfortable with our own company. We practiced love and compassion, striving to understand that life is a series of ups and downs. We delved deeper into our understanding of God's grace and mercy, and we learned to differentiate what truly matters in life.

Let's practice being open to sharing some of our experiences and life lessons with others, ensuring that our pain serves a purpose. On our path to success, it's essential to maintain good intentions and not view the success of others as a threat to our own journey. Recognize your worth and protect your thoughts, as you have the power to shape the decisions that define your life journey.

It's important to remember that when people hear the word "success," they often associate it solely with having a lot of money. Regardless of your current financial situation, there is someone out there who wishes they could be in your shoes. While financial stability is crucial for addressing life's needs, true success goes beyond wealth. It's about making progress and becoming a better version of yourself each day.

Your success is not defined by what someone else has achieved. It's your journey, your race, and your life; don't waste time looking at your neighbor's plate while your food is getting cold. In other words, stop comparing. When you find joy and passion in what you do, that's where true success awaits you.

There are a few things that I am always working on:

- Myself
- My faith
- My health
- My relationships
- My happiness
- My knowledge
- The understanding of my interest

- My style
- My wealth
- How I can make a difference

I aspire to inspire before I expire.

In 2009, I faced some challenging times, and I even contemplated giving up on the *Koze Fanm* show due to financial hardships. However, a turning point came when I was invited to a community event in Miami. I had the opportunity to address the audience after introducing myself and delivering my presentation.

Subsequently, as I reflected on this experience, I began to contemplate the true purpose of the *Koze Fanm* show. It dawned on me that it is vital to persevere and keep hope alive. One day, you will deeply appreciate yourself for not giving up, as you not only pursue your purpose but also positively impact the lives of others.

How Do You Make it Happen?

Take the initiative to start working towards the life you desire. Begin by taking the first step, keep moving forward, and witness your progress. Stay connected with the infinite spirit within you as you embark on your path to enlightenment. Sometimes, the most spiritual thing you can do is stay busy and do it joyfully. Pay attention, observe your thoughts, let go of what no longer serves you or what you can't control, and engage in activities that bring you joy. Summon the courage to persevere. Concentrate on the road ahead, never give up on yourself, and seek out endeavors that resonate with your soul. Set your intentions to find the solutions you desire. "Making it happen" involves balancing and harmonizing with both God and ourselves. We must gather the courage to balance our lives—striving for improved health, wealth, and spiritual connection.

To position ourselves for growth, it's imperative to receive training education, and engage in prayer. At some point, we must recognize that maturity requires taking responsibility for the trajectory of our lives and taking charge of our choices. Often, we say yes before fully comprehending what we are committing to, and we make adjustments along the way. This is why I am grateful I never gave up. The truth is life presents a continuous struggle, and it takes little effort to quit. While motivation ignited my journey, it was willpower that sustained it.

I am a Black, immigrant, and Haitian woman. My identity is riddled with doubts, contradictions, fears, and countless unanswered questions. I aspire to continue making a positive impact on my life and the lives of others, becoming my own kind of hero.

How do we survive conflicts? Conflict can be quite challenging at times. I firmly believe that when confronted with it, it's best to initiate the conversation sooner rather than later. Learning how to process our struggles can teach us valuable lessons and bring us closer to our authentic selves, fostering better relationships, whether with ourselves or others.

It's crucial to focus on personal growth and give yourself permission to be whoever you want to be. Pay attention to yourself, as energy follows where attention goes. It's time to free your mind from your own limiting beliefs in order to reach new heights and gain a deeper understanding. I refuse to allow myself to be held hostage, so I am committed to erasing those self-limiting beliefs. I know that I am a blessed child of God, perfectly and wonderfully made in His image.

I have learned to choose my path and strive for a better future, to stay true to myself, allowing myself to heal, and to trust in God's power. We must begin eliminating the invisible barriers imposed on us by religion, culture, or our parents, which prevent us from realizing our full potential. We have the power to control what works and what doesn't, enabling us to move forward.

When we gaze upon a painting, we often behold a magnificent work of art. We witness the culmination of thousands of brush strokes, skillfully blended colors, and intricate details that imbue depth, motion, and significance. Interestingly, we do not perceive each of these elements individually; rather, we perceive the final creation and the broader context.

Success mirrors this analogy. We admire accomplished individuals and their success, but we often remain unaware of the trials, countless hours, days, months, or even years they devoted to breathing life into the projects or businesses that have propelled them to their present success. The level of achievement I aspire to necessitates a distinct mode of thinking and action.

There was a period in my life when I worked as a part-time Creole interpreter. Our income needed to be higher because my ex-husband was a full-time student. During that time, we lived on a very tight budget, and my children were quite young. I used to sell handbags and custom jewelry from the trunk of my car, all while juggling my regular job to support the family.

This experience taught me the art of accessorizing, marketing, customer service, and more. It instilled in me a sense of style, enabling me to position myself as a certified image consultant and assist other women in looking and feeling fabulous.

Today, I am also a licensed real estate agent, which means I am qualified to sell anything from plots of land to high-rise properties. I still draw upon the skills I acquired during that transformative period many years ago, in addition to continually acquiring new ones.

I've experienced numerous uncomfortable situations, so I can confidently say that avoiding the process is not always the best solution! Elevate your grind; don't wait for opportunities to come to you. Instead, focus on creating the best version of yourself and never give up. Understand that growth only occurs through this journey. Take small steps and put in the work. Be humble in your victories and display courage during challenging times. As I embark on this journey to a new version of myself, I see my old self fading away.

Being a woman in business means leveraging your strengths and character to build a successful enterprise based on your unique personality and experiences. People are drawn to you and want to collaborate because your integrity and interests align with theirs.

While seeing the bigger picture is essential, don't underestimate the importance of zooming in on the small details of life's valuable lessons. Discover ways to create opportunities that align with your vision of the future. No matter what happens, never give up. Understand that every day is a fresh start, and have faith in God's plan for your life.

The journey to becoming the person you are today began at birth. Every experience has played a role in shaping your path, even seemingly insignificant moments and life-changing events. Some moments may have made you want to change the channel, while others required you to adjust the volume. Prioritize self-care to enhance your well-being, contentment, and personal growth. Dedicate time to engage in activities that hold personal significance and bring you genuine joy.

Navigating Different Seasons

Position yourself to find clarity and move forward. Sometimes, it's best to simply be still, be quiet, and let God fight your battles and orchestrate things in your favor. Don't fear starting over if necessary. Embrace reinvention and transformation as many times as needed. Each experience, lesson, and challenge deepens your consciousness and soul awareness. I hope that the painful moments in life have humbled us rather than hardened our hearts.

We must be mindful and actively seek ways to address the issues that cause us pain, aiming to resolve them and find inner light. Enjoy the different seasons in our lives, and summon the courage to start anew when required. What I've come to realize as I mature in life and faith is that there was a time when I kept myself incredibly busy, thinking it was the best way to avoid financial troubles. Now, I've learned the importance of slowing down to avoid danger.

Recently, I faced a situation where, in the past, I would have immediately addressed the issue. Instead, I found myself taking a more deliberate approach, carefully considering my thoughts, speaking slowly, and managing my emotions and breathing.

Psalm 139:

23 Search me, God, and know my heart; test me and know my anxious thoughts. 24 See if there is any offensive way in me, and lead me in the way everlasting.

Each moment is unique, but collectively, these moments are all yours. The experiences stack up and shape who you are. Remember to be thankful, think positive thoughts, strive to let go of worries, and learn to love, live, and appreciate yourself.

The sequence of events that has built my current reality is evidence of the interconnectedness of life itself. Although I often found myself all over the place, juggling many tasks, there is beauty in knowing that things tend to come together in ways beyond our control.

The beauty of life lies in the inevitability of change and growth. Life and business, like the seasons, remind us of how our lives shifted in 2020. That year presented an opportunity for me to rethink and restructure my life. Make the most of life and cherish every moment. Allow yourself to continue the journey with a different mindset.

To reach the "next level" in your life, you must be mentally and emotionally prepared. Taming the ego is a challenge. When God blesses you, pay close attention to your ego. I've learned a great deal over the years as opportunities have come and gone. Regardless of how hard you work or how successful you become, you can lose everything in a single day. Think about events like earthquakes in Haiti and other circumstances.

Improving our emotional intelligence is essential for success on our journeys and for manifesting the greatness within us.

Pray and maintain your faith, always wear a smile, celebrate your accomplishments, and keep showing up no matter how you feel. It's a symbol of hope and strength. Life is about growth and allowing change to happen while gaining a deeper understanding of the process. Our thoughts and emotions are often influenced by what we allow into our psyche.

Those of us who work in the media, especially in radio, often need to adjust the volume, whether it's the input or output, to ensure that we can hear and convey our messages effectively to our audience.

I've come to realize that adjusting the volume is just as crucial in our lives as we strive to find our frequency. This frequency helps us focus on valuable lessons, answer our calling, and walk the path that God has laid out for us.

One profound lesson I've learned about faith is that when God sees you making an effort, He will carry you through. I've prayed earnestly for God to grant me the strength, courage, and tools to write this book. I'm sharing my story to provide support, inspiration, and guidance to other women and single mothers who may be facing challenges similar to those I've overcome through faith.

Please take this opportunity to learn from my experiences, adjust your own volume, and allow your inner voice to shine brightly. Once you find that version of yourself that you've worked so hard to become, take good care of yourself and strive to be whole.

Reader Reflection

"Since you are my rock and my fortress, for the sake of your name, lead and guide me." - Psalm 31:3 (NIV)

"For you created my inmost being; you knit me together in my mother's womb.

I praise you because I am fearfully and wonderfully made; your works are wonderful, I know that fully well." - Psalm 139 (NIV)

"Trust in the LORD with all your heart and lean not on your own understanding; in all your ways submit to him, and he will make your paths straight. We should learn the little things and when the time comes, we'll be able to handle the big things in our lives." - Proverbs 3:5-6 (NIV)

Journal Prompts

1. Identify a major victory or proud moment in your life. Trace back to the root of this moment. Which circumstances, experiences, and events are "stacked" to bring this to fruition?

2. What are your best techniques to end an argument?

3. What are you afraid to do? What could you achieve if you face this fear and "do it terrified?"

4. What opportunities have you taken on that resulted in opening unexpected doors?

5. What opportunities have you turned down that resulted in opening unexpected doors?

Tips to Adjust the Volume

- Be the main character in your story

- Be fearless in the face of adversity

- Be open to knowledge

- Always think ahead

- Use your imagination

- Begin to think prosperous thoughts

- Remember where you come from

- Never lose sight of the destination

- Appreciate the light and the beauty that surrounds you

Enjoy a fulfilling life with more joy and more freedom. Live in the moment. This is your season of victory.

CHAPTER THREE
Path to Entrepreneurship

1 Peter 4:10 NIV

Each of you should use whatever gift you have received to serve others, as faithful stewards of God's grace in its various forms.

As a faith-based entrepreneur, I had to learn the basics of earning and what it means to be a person of service as a Christian woman. As mentioned in the book of Ecclesiastes, there is a time for everything: a time to sow, a time to nurture your crop, a time to harvest, and a time to rest. We need to strategize to find the right balance, focusing on finding solutions for ourselves and others and being good stewards. Whatever path we choose, as entrepreneurs, our businesses are personal because they affect all aspects of our lives.

Before I delve too deeply into the topic of entrepreneurship, I want to emphasize that entrepreneurs themselves don't fail; it's their companies that do. I've had many business ideas, some of which worked and some didn't. Entrepreneurship is a state of mind. Don't be afraid to take risks, don't give up easily, keep nurturing your creativity, and believe in your abilities. Be proactive in seeking knowledge and understanding because our imagination needs fuel.

From a very early age, I recall being as young as six years old when my mom would take me to her store every Saturday so I could work and witness how she conducted her business. They say, "If you hang around the barbershop long enough, sooner or later, you'll get a haircut." When I was twelve years old, I asked my mom to help me start my first business, and she did. After experimenting, don't be afraid to start over and explore different options. Use your past lessons and experiences to level up your thinking and knowledge. You are embarking on a new opportunity with the benefit of experience and an enhanced level of consciousness. The challenges you've overcome are your compass to guide you away from revisiting those same difficulties. Remember that God is aligning things in your favor.

A positive mindset can transform any hurdle into a wonderful opportunity in both life and business. Consider starting your business while still employed; this approach can save you a lot of time and reshape the entire landscape. You can dedicate your evenings from 5 PM to 9 AM to plan your dream business while maintaining your 9 AM to 5 PM job. It's crucial to cultivate a growth mindset before delving too deeply into this topic to foster the growth of your business. Keep in mind that the ultimate goal is to remain in the game and unlock new potential.

Your primary objective should be to work diligently to make progress and earn money, acquire the knowledge to preserve it and seek wisdom to multiply your resources.

If you find yourself in need of encouragement or self-accountability, remember the advice my mom used to give me: "Take your life seriously, Guylene." I vividly remember the excitement of registering "Global Solutions Agency" back in 2003, creating a business with immense potential for expansion. Many years later, my vision has become a reality, and that's because I took it seriously. Dream, envision, create, and refine the details as you progress. Even if you hear others suggesting they would have done it differently, remember that they are not in your shoes. The key is that you had a purpose before people offered their opinions. Focus on doing what is right and let it bring you peace; complete your mission.

When we're just starting out, things may seem complicated, and we often take whatever assignments come our way. However, it's essential to focus our marketing efforts on the target markets we most want to work with. As our business grows, we can build a team and consider giving up assignments that are less rewarding in order to devote more time to clients and projects that we find most fulfilling. This can be challenging because only you know who you are and how far you've come.

Remember that in due time, everything will fall into place. The same wind blows on all of us, and the same sun lights our days. Keep learning, take responsibility, and practice gratitude.

For me, entrepreneurship is a path to overcoming a poverty mindset. It involves maintaining a state of consciousness that aims to develop a high level of discipline, ultimately increasing our value. Continually assess yourself and ask what value you bring to people's lives, both through the services you offer and how you handle compensation. One doesn't have to be wealthy to start making a difference.

Recognize your weaknesses and leverage your strengths. In the early days of my painting business, I pursued a specific contract. When I went to bid on it, I found myself in a room full of men, with me being the only woman. Unfortunately, I had to walk away from the contract to protect my business, even though my bid was the lowest. However, I later realized that my company had better opportunities for growth and profit. It became clear to me that I was operating in a predominantly male-dominated industry. Looking back, I understood that the demands and requirements outlined in the project scope exceeded the low bid I proposed, and accepting the contract would have resulted in a loss. But this experience taught me more than just that. I learned that, as an entrepreneur, it's crucial to thoroughly research and ensure that the numbers add up, including checking for hidden expenses. Sometimes, what seems like an opportunity may not truly be one, and it's up to you to make that judgment.

In my role in the media and broadcasting business, I often reflect on my motivations. Have you taken the time to ask yourself why you want to be an entrepreneur? The path to entrepreneurship may not have been easy, but witnessing the fruits of my efforts, being able to provide for my family, and helping others make all the hard work worthwhile.

Utilize your gifts and talents to empower others. The decision to become an entrepreneur can be a significant one. As I'm still working on this journey myself, I have learned to be patient and to remember to be grateful when making a profit, whether it's big or small. There are a few questions to ask yourself when considering entrepreneurship to clarify your thoughts and intentions. These questions include:

- What are my choices?
- Where does my desire come from?
- Who do I want to become?
- What do I want to do?
- How is this going to affect my life?
- How can I maximize my potential?
- How am I going to make your money?
- What are the most significant actions I am willing to take to create the most desirable results now?
- What am I doing to get it?
- What am I doing to keep it?

When contemplating the path to entrepreneurship, the ultimate goal should encompass solving problems, creating freedom, and generating wealth. Many entrepreneurs aspire to increase their income while reducing their workload, although this isn't always the case. That's why I believe it's crucial to embark on a learning journey before expecting earnings; invest in honing your skills. To maximize your value, prioritize delivering tangible results over merely billing for your hours. Consider the wealth of knowledge and expertise you have amassed and leverage it to your advantage.

To succeed in your entrepreneurial pursuits, consistently focus on making sales and delivering services. Once you master this, you'll reach a point where you can work less and earn more. This experience will guide you in building something more sustainable.

In our quest for sustainable success, we must learn to persevere and enhance our lives. Countless opportunities remain undiscovered due to a lack of motivation. Fortunately, in today's era, we have limitless access to the power of the World Wide Web and Google. If you've been contemplating taking the leap into entrepreneurship, there's no better time than now.

However, it is a conscious choice we make, and making the right choice can pave the way for limitless opportunities, satisfying the needs of others and unlocking new possibilities. Establishing connections and networks is the key to success in the business world. Furthermore, it's crucial to surround yourself with supportive and knowledgeable individuals who can guide you towards promising avenues on the path to triumph. Remember that God has great plans for you; stay faithful and keep your eyes on the prize.

Choosing to be an entrepreneur also entails a commitment to constant innovation and learning new ways of doing things. If you aim to stay relevant and agile in the ever-changing landscape, your greatest asset will be your ability to navigate change, especially in today's fast-paced world. Simultaneously, any amount of money and success you enjoy won't hold much value if you don't take a moment to savor them. You've made many sacrifices to achieve these goals, so it's important to relish your achievements.

Sometimes, you have to start that business you've been dreaming of and planning in your head without having a business plan on paper. Just put on your thinking cap to create and innovate more effectively. Following your passion takes courage, so find encouragement, stay focused, and be resilient.

Starting a small business may sound exciting because you can be your own boss and invest your time and energy in something you are passionate about. However, there are many factors to consider before quitting your job and embarking on this venture.

Business owners need to be effective leaders who can motivate and inspire people with fresh ideas. Fortunately, we all possess creativity and leadership potential within us. To tap into it, we must silence our inner critic.

It's also crucial to acquire managerial skills, which necessitate continuous learning and ongoing practice. Make problem-solving a regular habit. If you practice it in your interactions with family, friends, and at work, you will eventually develop the qualities and skills required to become an exceptional business leader. Never cease your pursuit of knowledge.

Before we proceed, allow me to share some valuable questions that I wish I had answered before embarking on my entrepreneurial journey all those years ago:

1. What do I enjoy doing?
2. What's your plan? Do you solve, improve, resolve, or optimize?
3. What skills do I have?
4. What's your goal?
5. Why do I want to be an entrepreneur?
6. What would I spend my life doing if I had unlimited time, money, and influence?
7. What price am I willing to pay to be an entrepreneur?
8. What will I give up to follow my dream and make it work as an entrepreneur?
9. How long can I keep going before generating money from my business?
10. What to do to streamline efficiency and focus on building strong client relationships.

Becoming an entrepreneur is an ongoing journey in pursuit of a greater calling. Whenever I contemplate giving up, I pause and remind myself why I chose this path, which provides me with the strength to persevere. The opportunity to do what you love is empowering, offering lifelong freedom with a calculated risk or two. It immerses you in the excitement of innovation and creativity. The question is, are you ready to lead?

Being an entrepreneur makes me feel accomplished. It broadens my horizons and gives me a sense of purpose. As a female entrepreneur, I must maintain an unwavering focus to rise to the top and become the best businesswoman I can be. I aim to make the most of my available resources.

We can leverage our creativity and talents to bring about change and manifest our fortunes. We can share our skills, pursue our passions, and make a meaningful impact. In the meantime, we must strive for improvement as we learn. We need to commit ourselves to work diligently while also learning to work intelligently, paving the way for our success.

When I made the decision to transition into entrepreneurship after working regular jobs, my children were young, and I was divorced. It was then that I realized there's never a perfect time to become an entrepreneur, especially as a parent. Sometimes, you simply have to do what's necessary. Be courageous and keep moving toward your goals. I understand that it's not about what happens to you but how you respond when faced with adversity. I've invested in training across various areas to enhance my self-improvement, gain confidence, and acquire knowledge. This, in turn, has empowered me to serve others effectively and pursue my desired objectives with confidence.

No matter how busy or how many responsibilities you're juggling, it's crucial to make time for communication with the people who matter to you and to prioritize self-care.

For me, the ultimate goal is to find meaning. Even if you have well-defined objectives, there is no true endgame. You reach one milestone, and then you adapt. You encounter failure, and you adjust. Regardless of your personal definition of success, the journey will be marked by significant highs and painful lows that may leave you questioning everything. What I am certain of is that when I fail, it's because I've taken the courageous step of trying.

Over my many years on this journey, I've come to value the tough times, for it is in facing each challenge that a sense of suspense and chaos emerges, ultimately leading to a more extraordinary life adventure.

Reflecting back, it's evident that every challenge serves as a stepping stone toward a deeper sense of gratitude. Divine ideas never clash; they are harmonious. We are guided by a higher power and grace, knowing that the source of our abundance and provision comes from a divine source.

Business Ideas

Think both long-term and short-term and focus on the things that truly matter. Overcome distractions and continue pursuing the life you envision. The best approach is to decide what you want to do and believe in your abilities. Place more value on the choices we make. We must strive to balance our lives to achieve the quality of life we desire, enhancing the value we offer to both others and ourselves. Work diligently towards your dreams, and don't be too quick to give up when faced with challenges.

When searching for a good business idea, it's crucial to listen to ourselves and establish a scale for our achievements. Learn from our struggles to be more resilient and courageous, qualities for which Haitian people are well-known. Every idea begins as an experiment, requiring execution. Flexibility and knowing when to change course are essential in determining the necessity of staying on the same path. Always remember that circumstances change and evolve. Choosing a single business idea might seem overwhelming, particularly for multi-passionate individuals. However, don't let that deter you from starting. Let positivity and passion fuel your desires and actions, and anticipate that good things are on their way.

It's important to note that the best idea doesn't always win. Explore, remain open to different ideas, take the right course of action, and stick with what works best for you. Above all, consider a general idea you have in mind for your business venture and why these ideas are important to you. It's not just about mimicking someone else's success or randomly selecting an idea; it's about investing time in researching which opportunities align with your strengths and aspirations.

Begin by assessing your skills and talents. Consider the everyday issues faced by yourself, current co-workers, friends, or family members. Can you create a solution to address these challenges? Look for a niche with potential for growth and strive to meet that need. Be deliberate in crafting the reality you envision.

Once you have compiled a robust shortlist of ideas, it's time to narrow it down. Ask yourself why you want to start a business and identify which idea resonates most with your passion. What will motivate you to wake up every morning excited about the day and your life?

Funding the Dream

IT WAS A DEFINING MOMENT IN MY LIFE when I decided to enter the broadcasting field in 2006 and while I was on the verge of getting a divorce. I took the first step, and this adventure unfolded into something amazing. Don't let the size of your dream deter you from starting. You've probably heard that you need money to make money, and well, that's true most of the time. You're investing your time and money to bring your dream of the future to life. When you decide to pursue your business idea, it's important to consider the amount of funding and time required to establish the company. Additionally, factor in the future budget necessary to sustain and expand the business.

There are multiple approaches to consider. Self-funding or using OPM (Other People's Money) is a viable path. It can be risky, but it can help you avoid taking out loans you may struggle to repay. Another option is to approach investors, share your business plan with them, and hope they will believe in your business's potential for success and be willing to invest in your dream.

Advertise your business

Ensure that your words align with your actions and maintain a forward-thinking perspective on innovation. Proactively engage in problem-solving, as customers are more likely to share negative experiences than positive ones. Develop an effective marketing plan that is both user-friendly and culturally sensitive. In today's digital age, there are numerous opportunities to promote and showcase our business. Dedicate time to learn and implement these strategies, and prioritize integrity, honesty, and reliability. Continuously seek out new ways to enhance your customers' experience.

Customer service plays a pivotal role in a business's growth and success. There is no one-size-fits-all approach when it comes to finding the right strategy that works. For a business to thrive, it must attract and retain customers, as satisfied customers not only return but also refer others. It's crucial to identify your niche market and strategically target them. I once came across the analogy that if you want to hunt tigers, you must venture where the tigers reside. Strive to create a memorable experience for them.

Being actively present and engaged with your audience will enable you to establish a stronger connection. Explore various methods to connect with your target audience, expanding your reach. Social media has significantly facilitated this process, offering a cost-effective means to do so. However, it's equally essential for every business to have a website that potential customers can visit and engage with.

Other advertising avenues include radio, such as the Koze Fanm show, local TV, newspaper ads, and paid digital media. Whichever advertising route you choose, it's essential to assess your Return on Advertising Spend (ROAS) to determine which method performs the best for you. This analysis will guide your future marketing investments effectively.

Growing and Building with Grace

"Don't let your food get cold while worrying about what's on other people's plates; stop comparing. Fear must be overcome repeatedly. To help your business grow, update your vision to ensure you are on the right track. If you're not headed in the right direction, this will provide you with the insight to pivot and adjust your projected cash flow and progress.

Always remember that business involves buying, selling, and trading. If your business is starting to expand, it might be time to consider building the right team. Accept responsibility, engage in continuous learning, invest in yourself, understand your why, and, most importantly, celebrate your victories along the way, whether they are big or small. The path to entrepreneurship is about the journey, not the destination.

My entrepreneurial journey began early in my life because I became aware of the value of a dollar at a young age. In elementary school, I asked my mother for extra money, and she wanted to know what it was for. So, at the age of eight, I started saving my lunch money and asked the housekeeper to buy me meals from restaurants.

Having a bit of extra spending money was enjoyable, so I began saving extra for when I would travel with my mom. Waiting to get home to have food at restaurants worked for a few years, but skipping lunch was not ideal. So, when I was around 12 years old, I decided to start my own business to earn more.

My mom used to design and distribute fabric, selling wholesale textiles. She sourced fabric in New York and Panama to sell in Haiti, and she was locally known for her unique designs and textures. When I told her about my business venture aspirations, she taught me how to create and sell scrunchies for hair.

At the time, scrunchies were becoming a trendy item, but they mostly came in black or white. The scrunchies I sold were made from various kinds of fabrics I obtained from my mother's textile store, featuring a variety of bright and neon colors. I affectionately called them "happy colors." I began selling them at school and on Sundays after church.

With my own business and savings from gifts I had received, I could accumulate enough money to spend when we traveled to New York and buy things for myself. I was particularly interested in photography at that time, so some of my first significant purchases included an Olympus camera, a Walkman, and a watch.

These three pieces of equipment provided me with a sense of freedom. The Walkman allowed me to listen to any songs I liked at the volume that suited me best. I consider myself fortunate to have been able to dance to music that I enjoyed.

My business continued to grow for the next two years until we relocated to the United States. I began attending East Orange High School in New Jersey. I stopped selling scrunchies and started selling jewelry. On weekends, I would take the train to Manhattan on Broadway in New York City to purchase my pieces, which I would then sell to girls at school and church to help them accessorize. After another two years, we uprooted once again and returned to Haiti.

Upon our return to Haiti, I turned 16 years old. One day, I accompanied my mom to the seamstress. I wasn't interested in going inside with her, so I hung out in the car. As I looked around, a large factory caught my eye. The factory was manufacturing underwear. I began purchasing underwear in bulk, washing and packaging them to sell to my classmates and other teenagers. I continued doing this throughout high school, and it proved to be quite lucrative at the time.

As I transitioned into adulthood, I gained valuable business experience by working alongside my mom. I pursued formal education in bookkeeping, but life took a different turn when I moved to the United States. I initially lived in New Jersey before making South Florida my permanent residence in 1997.

During this period, I continued assisting my mother with her business. However, she decided to close the used clothing import-export department, which left me with limited responsibilities. I needed to find new opportunities to contribute to my family's finances. At that time, my ex-husband was a full-time student, and my children were very young, so I had no choice but to support them. This led me to take on the role of a medical interpreter for workman's compensation cases.

Transitioning into this role brought about significant financial challenges. We struggled to pay rent and maintain a roof over our heads. This challenging period illuminated how financial difficulties could strain relationships and make us appreciate the things we often take for granted in the absence of financial stability.

I want to share a particular scenario from my life when my car broke down. At that time, my children were very young, and commuting from North Miami to the Aventura Mall for work became quite challenging. I was employed as a sales associate at Macy's, and one day, I was presented with an opportunity for a promotion and a raise to work in a different department.

During the interview for the promotion, the manager asked me to make a commitment that I would never be late if I were to get the position. Being true to myself, I told her I needed some time to think about it. My hesitation stemmed from the fact that my children were still very young and most days, I relied on taking the bus to and from work. This was because my ex-husband and I were sharing a single car, and I couldn't guarantee punctuality until I could afford to fix my broken-down vehicle or purchase a new one. In South Florida, where public transportation was not the most reliable option for daily commuting, I had to be honest about my situation.

Soon after this encounter, I began searching for job opportunities in "The Flyer," a classified ad magazine popular in the late nineties. As I perused the classified ads, I stumbled upon one that piqued my interest. I called the provided number, and they informed me that they were looking for actresses with no prior experience required. They offered a wage of $25 per hour, which seemed reasonable to me at the time.

The person on the other end of the line asked if I had any acting experience. I mentioned that I had taken drama classes in high school and had participated in some acting at my church. However, he proceeded to inquire if I knew what a "golden shower" was, a term I was unfamiliar with. In response, he conveyed that he didn't think I qualified for the job based on my lack of knowledge about that term.

This particular incident prompted me to turn to God, whom I refer to as "my Infinite Source," seeking patience, guidance, and clarity to navigate the challenges I was facing during those difficult times.

Despite the numerous moves, transitions, and adjustments I experienced during my early years as an entrepreneur, one constant remained: the passionate entrepreneurial spirit that always resided within me. I persevered through years of hard work, eventually rekindling my journey as a creative entrepreneur with Global Solutions Agency, all with the goal of better serving my community.

The Radio Business

The Koze Fanm show taught me so much in life. I learned to manage my energy and time, create momentum, and be more spontaneous. My primary goal was to start a program to connect the community with resources to help them progress. I realized that the best way to accomplish this was to use the airwaves. One of the business endeavors I embarked on was Koze Fanm, my radio show, which launched in 2006. Producing and hosting the show taught me the importance of discovering a unique niche and standing out from the crowd. It also helped me improve my communication skills and maintain a calm demeanor. Through my experience, I identified my strengths and weaknesses.

Additionally, I learned that most fears eventually dissipate. Radio is a highly creative and expressive medium. Hosting a radio show is also a business that many listeners and fans may need to realize. Like any entrepreneur, I've also faced many challenges that have molded me into the person I am today. That's why I've spent so much time learning about the radio industry, my specific audience, and how I can best serve them. Sometimes, it gets challenging, but it's also been gratifying.

Once I reached a point where I felt comfortable and had mastered my craft as a radio broadcaster, I began to truly enjoy being a producer. Controlling the soundboard, selecting music, and choosing discussion topics allowed me to adjust my mood and better connect with both my guests and my audience. It's fascinating to witness how my energy can have such a profound impact on people.

An essential aspect of my broadcasting journey is that I dove in head-first. I was immensely enthusiastic about starting my venture, which led me to overlook the importance of the business side of things. While I did have some experience in communications and a general understanding of the purpose of my show, I began without a solid plan. Consequently, the initial years proved more challenging than necessary, and my lack of business knowledge led to avoidable setbacks.

There were moments when I came close to giving up, several times, in fact. However, during one of these moments, I had a pivotal conversation with my friend, Rene Godefroy, that completely changed my perspective on time management. When I shared the difficulties I faced as a woman in the radio industry, he asked, "Isn't your passion centered around assisting individuals who are dealing with obstacles?" It's incredibly valuable to be reminded of our purpose by a trusted source from time to time.

He pointed out that my purpose for being on the radio was never about money or recognition; it was about reaching the masses, helping people overcome challenges, changing lives, and providing access to opportunities. My perception shifted almost immediately. As they say, "Attitude creates altitude." I had to take my own advice and persevere through the struggles at times. I needed to adopt a new approach, understanding that I could bring something fresh by simply being myself and allowing God to use me.

The relationships we build can either make or break our businesses. It's crucial to be mindful of who we grant access to. I've learned the importance of staying true to my word to build trust and establish meaningful professional relationships. To maintain a solid professional rapport, it's essential to keep emotions out of business matters and remain attentive and level-headed.

Furthermore, maintaining these relationships requires avoiding making assumptions. While it's essential not to get too personal, we must remember that people have things going on in their lives that we can't always see. Avoid making unfounded assumptions, as they can lead to trouble.

Another key to maintaining professional relationships is always giving your best effort. Consistently show up and put your best foot forward. This approach not only elevates your own success but also contributes to the success of those around you.

The concept is to lead a life in harmony, both with ourselves and others. Now that I'm older, everything is beginning to make sense. I eventually realized the importance of finding harmony with my audience. It was essential to take the time to understand why people initially tuned in to the radio.

Radio can evoke powerful emotions, but it also serves a practical purpose. While I excelled at the emotional aspect, I struggled with the practical side. To improve the balance of my show, I enlisted the help of a journalist to provide a segment covering local and Haitian news.

Incorporating this news segment helped me develop a better structure for my show, one that I still use today. I begin each show with an introduction and some inspiration. The inspirational segment typically includes tips to live by or a quote of the day.

Following that, I play a gospel song before transitioning into a quick commercial break, followed by the news segment and community announcements. If I have guests, they have their time to shine after the news segment concludes. I open the lines for interaction. I conclude the show on a positive note with the music I'm currently enjoying. Since my show is a talk show, I'm not confined to any specific music genre, and I always encourage my listeners to invest in themselves for a brighter tomorrow.

My show is primarily family-friendly, but at times, we delve into more sensitive topics such as divorce, parenting, sexuality, and more. Despite our discussions of challenging subjects, the Koze Fanm show is designed to be a beacon of light in the darkness. I aim to assist my listeners in navigating difficult times as if I were a steadfast friend or companion. I prefer the topics I discuss with my guests to spark dialogues among my listeners and their loved ones.

Even after I found my rhythm, I continued to face another battle. It felt as though I was in competition with other radio programmers as if we were dueling over limited and scarce resources. I have come to understand that success is within everyone's reach, and it's not about being superior to others. Instead, it's about recognizing and fully utilizing your strengths.

Reflecting on that conversation with Rene, I once again realigned my focus. This required me to set aside my ego and reconnect with my original purpose. As I made that shift, new opportunities emerged, and new horizons came into view. But here's a little secret: the fear of failure never completely vanishes. Even today, as an entrepreneur, I keep flipping the coin until it lands in my favor.

During my time working at the City of North Miami and the CRA as a community outreach advisor and liaison, my boss proposed a specific campaign for first-time homebuyers that had been ongoing since 2007. We aimed to disseminate information to residents in Miami-Dade County who were purchasing their first homes and might be eligible for affordable housing resources and home retention programs. Some funds were available to assist them with their down payment to qualify for a mortgage. Initially, I had planned to share it exclusively on my show, but I soon realized the immense value of this information and knew it had to reach a broader audience.

I reached out to other radio programmers on various stations to inquire if they would be interested in discussing this resource on their shows. The common response I received was, 'How much does it pay?' These radio programmers had a valid point. Participation required financial support, making it logical for them to request airtime in exchange for promoting initiatives like this. I then contacted Tony Crapp Sr., who was the executive director at the time. The board was able to allocate some funding to promote the program through radio advertising.

As I was a contractor with the City of North Miami and the CRA, I couldn't execute these deals as an agency. Nevertheless, this experience planted the seed that would eventually grow into Sak Pase Media, the media agency I still operate today.

This opportunity opened doors for me within the radio industry. Other programmers began to accept and respect me, treating me more like a colleague than a competitor.

I owe a debt of gratitude to Chenet Nerette, who gave me the confidence to broadcast my show across multiple radio stations and online streaming platforms. I used WSRF to connect to these platforms and SakPaseMedia.com for live online streaming. While at the Hot 105 studio with Rodney Baltimore, I observed him simultaneously working on the Tom Joyner Morning Show and another syndicated program. When I asked him about syndication, he kindly explained it to me, inspiring the idea of syndicating the Koze Fanm show. My goal has always been to disseminate valuable information and resources to a broader audience, and I'm immensely grateful for the progress I've made toward achieving this goal. I thank God for this incredible opportunity.

The "Koze Fanm" show is currently being broadcast on numerous online platforms and seven different stations across South Florida, as well as Orlando, Boston, and Connecticut, with live streaming available online. Despite the diversity of these locations and the fact that my listeners abroad reside in various circumstances, we can all unite through the mission of my show: to spread happiness, positivity, and opportunities to everyone we encounter. Our shared aspiration for personal growth and well-being is what binds us all together.

Tips to Start a Business

Starting a business is a significant undertaking, however rewarding. The best Bible verse for entrepreneurs to help any business succeed is found in **Matthew 7:7 (NIV): "Ask and it will be given to you; seek and you will find; knock and the door will be opened to you."**

What it ultimately comes down to is that entrepreneurship involves providing solutions for financial exchange. While I still have more goals to achieve, I am continuously dedicated to the hard work required for my business. Over the years of being an entrepreneur in the broadcasting and media industry, I've gained valuable insights about both myself and the intricacies of the business world.

As I mentioned earlier, the first step is to examine your intentions. Focus on becoming the change you wish to see rather than solely concentrating on potential income. Go deeper and ask yourself whether you would still want to be in this business if you were faced with adversity or challenges. An idea might sound promising in theory, but it must align with the context of your life.

One of the most fundamental aspects of business is offering a solution to a problem. Clarify what you have to offer and determine the true value of your offering. Conduct research to gain a better understanding of the audience you will cater to and explore existing alternative options.

Once you've established clear intentions and identified your offering, take the necessary steps to formalize your business on paper. Investigate local guidelines and regulations to determine the requirements for incorporation, licensing, and ensuring the legal status of your business entity. This proactive approach will help you avoid legal issues, and having everything sorted out in advance will simplify matters when tax season arrives.

Another crucial aspect to consider when starting out is your personal and business finances. Calculate the initial costs required to launch your business and create realistic projections for when you can expect to turn a profit. Evaluate your current personal financial situation and determine how much you can comfortably invest. Are there any sacrifices you'll need to make, and are there any you're unwilling to make? Do you require financial support through a business loan or an investor?

One risky step that many people take is quitting their jobs to start a business. Quitting your job to focus on growing your business is a different scenario; think it through thoroughly before submitting your two-week notice. Depending on your needs and responsibilities, it might be a good idea to maintain stability and responsibility during the initial years of entrepreneurship. Understand that starting a business involves risks, and keep your objectives clear. Don't assume that you'll achieve the same success as someone else just because they did. You must be prepared to work hard, even if it means working from 9 to 5 and then dedicating your evenings from 6 to 10 to your entrepreneurial dream. You can be both an employee and an entrepreneur simultaneously, and you should adjust accordingly.

I mention these risks not to discourage you but to emphasize the importance of being realistic. Running a business can be incredibly rewarding, but it may also entail personal and financial setbacks. Be prepared for disappointments, and if you genuinely believe in your venture, never give up.

As the world continually changes, we must adapt to the new normal. It's crucial to secure financial stability for ourselves and future generations. So, stay focused, stay informed, and embrace the journey. Take action and practice your passion.

Things I Wish I Knew

Life is constantly changing:

-My priorities will change.

-My relationship will change.

-My financial status will change

-My values will change.

-My knowledge will change.

-My interest will change.

-My mindset will change.

IT'S IMPORTANT TO KNOW THAT WE ARE BEAUTIFUL.

Know where to draw the line. In life, we must be careful about whom we share our thoughts and secrets with because, during the season of our growth, some may reveal the intimate conversations we've had with them to demonstrate their former closeness to us. Sometimes, they even fabricate stories about us. The best way to care for others is to care for ourselves first and be our own best friend. We are often advised to keep pushing, work harder, and take things more seriously. However, we must also learn to take time to breathe, relax, refuel, and reflect for a moment. I've come to realize that I can say no to others and yes to myself.

If we want to elevate our lives to a higher level, we must develop self-respect, compassion, and a certain level of consciousness. We must also stop fixating on the wrong things. I had to put this philosophy into practice to move toward a happier and more fulfilling life. The key is to remain open to discovering new ways of adjusting.

One game-changing realization was that I had to prioritize my well-being ahead of others. I couldn't fully serve others if I wasn't serving myself first. You can't give even a drop of effort or energy to anyone else if you're running on empty. Emotional balance is profoundly important, and we all possess the power to shift our moods.

I recognized that destructive emotions were causing some of my suffering, so I am constantly working to eliminate them from my mind. It's crucial to avoid dwelling on negative thoughts related to people, business, or relationships. Instead, ask for guidance from God to help you become a source of peace.

As I mentioned earlier, I should have taken my radio business more seriously. I dove in headfirst without a clear idea of what to do. Honestly, there's so much I wish someone had told me, as it would have made the process much smoother from the start. Establishing visibility and having a strong voice is crucial for positioning oneself effectively. After a few years on the air, my mom pointed out, "This radio hobby is costing you a lot." She asked if I was trying to build a business or simply treating the radio show as a hobby. If it were a business, I needed to adjust and ensure that I covered the three essential business aspects: buying, selling, and trading. I was buying airtime as a radio programmer, but I wasn't selling or trading it. I should have been selling airtime to individuals or brands interested in featuring on my show. Compensation could have been monetary or in exchange for other services. In either case, it motivated me to become more serious about what I was doing and how I approached my radio broadcasting business.

That said, the best advice I can offer to new entrepreneurs is to take their business seriously. If you don't take your business seriously, others won't take you seriously either. When there's such a disconnect, people will start expecting freebies, and this can become a vicious cycle that holds you back unless you intentionally address it.

I previously emphasized the significance of having a business structure, but it's equally important to maintain it. Develop a plan that fosters success and adhere to it while staying focused on critical matters.

Truly knowing and understanding your audience, as well as the industry you're in, is another vital lesson. It's crucial to consider the tactics and strategies required to assist your audience effectively. This requires mindfulness and thoughtful planning.

Depending on the market you want to target, your approach should vary. Even after identifying your target audience, you must continuously research and engage with them to understand their current needs. This understanding will prove invaluable in all aspects of branding, marketing, and advertising.

Take the "Koze Fanm" show, for instance. It's designed for anyone who can appreciate women's issues, which is how it earned its name. Initially, some people believed my show would exclusively cater to women and might denigrate men. However, women's issues often intersect with family issues, which also affect men. I've hosted numerous shows and segments that appealed more to men than women because I recognize that everything I do ultimately relates to the challenges women face.

WEARING MANY HATS

Proverbs 31:31: "Honor her for all that her hands have done. Let her works bring her praise."

You don't need to have everything figured out to find happiness. Being grateful for what you have now positions you in a better place to receive even more. Have the courage to step into your greatness. I've learned not to focus on closed doors but to look for open windows. Many of us aspire to have our own businesses, but are we driven by the right motives? Are we in business solely for the exchange of money or for the exchange of value? As I mentioned earlier, being dedicated to the hustle and being willing to work hard is imperative. As an entrepreneur, I've worn many hats and taken on various roles. My mom even used to chide me for doing too much. Well, guess what? I became a side hustle pro.

At times, it felt like I was all over the place, but everything I was doing was connected to the bigger picture. I've remained hands-on with my different business endeavors, making time management and organization crucial. I allocate different days for various businesses and projects to ensure I give my best effort to each one. I believe in diversifying income, so even though it can be challenging, I've had to be careful not to spread myself too thin.

While my radio show has been one of my primary businesses, I've had to become strategic over the years to create time for my other projects. For instance, syndicating my show and expanding to multiple platforms allowed me to invest less time while broadening my reach and amplifying my impact. Like many entrepreneurs, adapting to the "new normal" in the wake of COVID-19 presented numerous challenges. Transitioning to a virtual environment made it challenging to continue with some of my endeavors that thrived in face-to-face settings, leading to struggles for some of my businesses during the pandemic.

The strain of the pandemic brought me to a tipping point. As I grow older, I now value my peace and sanity more than the chaos and busy schedules I used to enjoy. Therefore, I continually make necessary adjustments to ensure that everything I do aligns with my current reality and makes the most sense. Sometimes, you need to scale down and adapt your involvement based on what makes the most sense at the moment. Although I believe that business can offer rewards beyond just financial gain, I recognize that time is incredibly precious. Once time is spent, it cannot be reclaimed, so it's crucial to learn how to use our time wisely.

Through my years of experience in various roles, I've gained valuable insights that I would like to share with new entrepreneurs. It's essential to focus on one venture and master it before moving on to the next. This approach creates a solid foundation for building a profitable and sustainable business. This advice is rooted in my own experience, and I regret not applying it earlier in my career.

As you learn and grow, being patient with yourself is crucial. Despite our difficulties, failures, and conflicts, we can still find beauty and inner radiance. My goal is to discover a guiding light that leads me to my own version of the Promised Land. For me, this means making peace with myself, finding my sense of freedom, and helping others find their own light. Instead of fixating on blame, let's search for lessons, solutions, and healing, and let's keep moving forward.

Over the years, as I've encountered difficulties and challenges, I turned to God for support. I learned that assistance doesn't always come from those closest to us. However, God has a way of bringing people together to aid us in fulfilling our purpose. In business, prioritizing collaboration and building connections with others is more significant than engaging in competition. Competition can lead to exhaustion or even mental strain.

As we navigate through life, we inevitably encounter setbacks and challenges. Nevertheless, our values are not solely determined by external factors such as time, space, or material possessions. Instead, they are shaped by our responses to these experiences, our mindset, our sense of gratitude, and our personal growth. Ultimately, our capacity to find fulfillment in these aspects propels us forward.

These elements can either make or break us, depending on how we react and rebound from related situations. Failure provides us with insights into where we can improve and how we can pivot or adapt. Our true selves are revealed through conflicts in any situation, relationship, or dynamic.

At times, it's valuable to recognize how other people's egos and greed have led to their failures. You can forge your own path to success based on these observations and lessons. Personal failures can serve as a catalyst for your growth as an entrepreneur. From my own experiences, I've learned that a lack of preparation sets you on a course towards failure. Insufficient preparation leads to tardiness, subpar presentations, and missed opportunities.

One example is that you can't afford to be late when you're traveling or trying to catch a flight. If you aren't prepared, you will miss your flight. For instance, when traveling, buying a last-minute ticket can lead to higher trip costs, and it can also result in missing meetings, other engagements, or even your destination. This was a situation that occurred too often for me when I was younger. However, I've improved over time through better planning and organization.

Conflict is not always avoidable, but it may be wise to refrain from arguing with others, as not all disputes can be resolved immediately or through verbal communication. The same applies to internal conflicts. However, it's often best to avoid stirring up trouble and, instead, seek forgiveness and distance yourself from conflicts since most battles are won or lost before any fighting occurs. If your spouse or friend is upset and taking it out on you, remind them that it's not a matter of "me" against "you" but rather "both of us" against the problem. It can be helpful to address the source of the problem and find its origin.

It's also vital to consciously control your time, place, and mood before entering into any conversation. This is something that I continuously work on myself—self-control and self-mastery. Everyone should seek their own approaches to managing self-image and self-discipline.

I realize that both failure and conflict can be dealt with by setting boundaries and limitations on what I can no longer accept. I continue to learn, grow, and evolve while restructuring my company.

Several years ago, my friend McGarrett, who is an insurance broker, encouraged me to obtain my life and health insurance license. I followed his advice, and when I resigned from my position as a community liaison and outreach specialist at the city of North Miami, I expanded my business by offering insurance products. In my view, life insurance is the most effective and affordable way for low-income individuals and families to secure a lasting legacy and make a positive impact on their family's lives.

One day, after hosting the show, my colleague Gilbert suggested that I explore the possibility of becoming a Medicare representative. He pointed out that seniors have a fondness for my infectious laughter when they listen to me on the Koze Fanm show. Over the years, I've shared valuable resources on the radio, and every time patients tune in or watch the show, they inquire about me during their doctor's visits at Preferred Family Care. They also seek my services at several medical centers in the community. Additionally, I co-produced and co-hosted the TV show "Priorite Sante" Health First with Dr. Patrick Romeus for "Preferred Family Care."

These additions to my business have created significant opportunities for Koze Fanm show listeners to gain insights into leaving a lasting legacy for their children without straining their finances. This endeavor has provided access to new resources that enable me to improve the lives of my listeners. I always encourage them to "invest in themselves for a better tomorrow," which has also become my signature sign-off for the show.

A couple of years later, during the pandemic, I made the most of my time in that situation by obtaining my real estate license and acquiring several other certifications. It also taught me the value of slowing down in life to make progress, as they say, "Downtime is prep time." We can find opportunities for growth in such situations, so it's crucial to seize them. This is how we develop as individuals and ultimately succeed. Always strive for self-improvement.

Reader Reflection

"Jabez cried out to the God of Israel, 'oh, that you would bless me and enlarge my territory! Let your hand be with me, and keep me from harm so that I will be free from pain.' And God granted his request." - 1 Chronicles 4:10 (NIV)

"Who is wise and understanding among you? Let them show it by their good life, by deeds done in the humility that comes from wisdom." - James 3:13 (NIV)

"So as to walk in a manner worthy of the Lord, fully pleasing to him, bearing fruit in every good work and increasing in the knowledge of God." - Colossians 1:10 (NIV)

"Ship your grain across the sea; after many days you may receive a return. Invest in seven ventures, yes, in eight; you do not know what disaster may come upon the land." - Ecclesiastes 11:1-2 (NIV)

Journal Prompts

Entrepreneurship means providing solutions to others in exchange for values.

1. What does being successful mean to you? We need to focus on defining success our way. Once you know that answer, you can go after your dreams.
2. Why do you want to start your business?
3. Who can you serve with this business?
4. Are you ready and willing to invest your time and energy into this business?
5. What are your business goals?

Tips to Adjust the Volume

- Be open to learning new things.
- Have a plan and strategy in place for economic growth.
- Tap into your unofficial network.
- Expand your network with other people who have already succeeded.
- Be willing to evolve and put your creativity cap on.
- Find your element and discover your passion.
- Above all, have a positive outlook on your business.

CHAPTER FOUR

The Koze Fanm Network:
The Pathway to My Mission

The Koze Fanm Network helped me redefine my purpose and gave me a sense of fulfillment. In 2006, I began using radio as a platform to serve. My mission and aspiration are to be a source of hope and make a difference in people's lives. I had to take a leap of faith and go for it. So, I took a chance, and it worked. You already possess the potential to be great. By taking action, I conveyed my idea and started the Koze Fanm show, which eventually became a syndicated program. I adjusted my faith to understand God's plan for my life. With consistency, something average can be transformed into something excellent. The radio business helped me gain a lot of understanding and provided me with access to many wonderful connections and opportunities. I aligned my values with actions, founded the Koze Fanm show, and turned the idea into reality. Finding your purpose is a personal journey that is constantly evolving. When I left my state job in 2006 as a court interpreter to become an entrepreneur and establish the Koze Fanm show, it felt like a shift from a career to a calling. I juggled many jobs as a single mother while pursuing my dream of becoming an entrepreneur. I worked as a freelancer, interpreter/translator, community liaison consultant, painting contractor, voice-over and production consultant, and media strategist for politicians and organizations. I hustled because I wanted to follow my passion for serving, producing, and hosting the Koze Fanm show, even though it wasn't making enough money to support myself and my children.

As it is stated in the Bible, "I can do all things through Christ who strengthens me." Connecting people with opportunities has always been, and continues to be, my passion. What meaningful initiative are you currently undertaking in your life? This invaluable and significant endeavor has also provided me with a purpose, allowing me to voice my thoughts and create an outlet to share my insights. Being a Christian woman, I prayed for guidance on how I could better serve and discover my purpose before I turned 33. Numerous ideas came to me all at once, and finding my mission and purpose became paramount to me.

It all began with the Koze Fanm syndicated show. I embarked on the journey of becoming a media host in 2006. It was far from easy, but I pushed forward despite feeling scared, alone, financially strained, and exhausted. That same year, I also became a single mother. However, I never gave up. This experience served as a valuable lesson in understanding the law of vibration, and I continue to practice and refine it. Through this process, I have learned the significance of confronting my fears, persisting, and discovering my authentic voice, freedom, and power. We must pray for success, take action, and exercise patience.

Even though I may not be providing my listeners with a monetary gift, I can still assist them by sharing my knowledge and experiences to help secure their financial future. Furthermore, acquiring various certifications and licenses will broaden my opportunities to serve my listeners more effectively and tangibly. Sharing resources allows us to evolve, grow, and progress together.

When you align your work with your love for serving others, many doors will open to joy, peace, and abundance in ways you can't even imagine.

I've embarked on many unexpected journeys, but they have taken me to some beautiful places. I believe God is guiding me, even when I can't see the path ahead. Through these experiences, I've learned that persistence helps us realize our strength and ability to achieve our goals. Even seemingly impossible tasks can be accomplished when we try. Staying true to ourselves throughout the process helps us discover the message we are meant to share. So, if there is something you want to do, go for it. The path ahead is unpredictable.

God blessed me with the gift of creativity, and it has enabled me to build a brand, foster a community, and establish a platform that has opened doors to various opportunities. One of the unique ways I connect with the Haitian community is by bringing in diverse guests and covering a range of topics. I have consciously developed my skill set to better serve this community. Given the current landscape, adaptability and efficiency are essential in navigating change. I have striven to enhance my qualifications and nurture my creativity with the goal of leaving a lasting legacy and creating something magnificent. Through this journey, I've come to understand that optimism unveils pathways to remarkable opportunities, and positive energy instills confidence.

At times, the end of one chapter marks the beginning of something truly great. In my role as an interpreter, I bore witness to numerous injustices and discovered how a lack of knowledge could hinder one's freedom. Over the past fifteen years, I have had the privilege of serving as a bridge, using my voice to help people access information and resources to improve their lives and those of their families.

As a woman in broadcasting, I faced the challenge of setting boundaries with my audience. On occasion, I had to cut certain comments short. I also applied the same boundary-setting with other radio hosts, many of whom were men who made inappropriate comments, often thinking they were humorous. Establishing these boundaries was not always easy because I desired to be liked, but it was a necessary step. In such situations, we must ask ourselves whether we would prefer to be loved or respected.

Never give up on your dreams of becoming a better version of who you want to be. It's tough to wait, but even tougher to live with regret. It's important to realize that lasting change doesn't happen overnight, whether it involves changing habits or personal growth.

When I was a young girl, attending church and learning about the life of Jesus Christ, I always wondered what my calling was. I decided to use my talents and God-given gifts to make a difference, and now I employ those gifts to be the change I want to see. One way I accomplished this was by becoming more involved in helping my Haitian community and using the radio as a tool for change.

I often ask myself, 'What is the magic glue that holds our community together?' I believe the answer lies in our love for our country, Haiti. But what are we doing here as a diaspora? While living here, we still maintain our interests, personalities, hopes, dreams, and fears. The Haitian culture's motto is 'L'Union Fait la Force,' or 'Stronger Together.'"

I initiated the *Koze Fanm* radio show with the intention of serving my community and fostering unity among people. My mission on the *Koze Fanm* show was, and continues to be, to provide information that can enhance people's lives. While working as a Creole interpreter in the court system, I noticed that many resources were not reaching the Haitian community due to language barriers. Listening to some of the Haitian radio shows at that time, I realized that I could introduce a unique element, incorporating humor, inspiration, and valuable information to empower my audience.

When I established the show, my goal was to offer valuable knowledge and resources to help people not only survive but thrive. I believe that everyone should have equal access to certain privileges, such as health and life insurance to build generational wealth, government assistance for starting a business or buying a home, and resources for adult education, grants, and parenting. Additionally, I aimed to emphasize the importance of fathers actively participating in their children's lives.

I have faith in the work I'm doing, utilizing the tools at my disposal to make a meaningful impact in people's lives and connect great ideas with strong values.

Koze Fanm Network isn't just my passion; it's also my mission that extends beyond the confines of the radio and TV show. I see myself as both a leader and an artist, known for my laughter, spontaneity, and fashion sense. Each day presents an opportunity for me to let my light shine and connect with others from the heart. When I'm live on the radio, it's a chance to infuse new energy into the space, which I then apply to my daily life. The *Koze Fanm* brand has evolved into an award-winning radio and TV show recognized by BOMA (Black Owned Media Alliance), along with hosting events, offering merchandise, and publishing a magazine. This collective experience is now contributing to the content of the Adjust the Volume book series.

Koze Fanm serves as a platform for communication with both women and men, aiming to empower families through broadcasting and various forms of outreach. It's more than just a one-woman show.

Women's issues are, to me, societal issues that demand attention. These matters hold significant importance in my heart. God has crafted the female body in an awe-inspiring manner, capable of bearing children. However, it's essential to clarify that when I mention "women's issues," I'm encompassing all aspects of life that impact human existence, whether directly or indirectly. This extends beyond familial concerns.

In areas unrelated to the family, women often find themselves facing choices between being loved and being respected. As a woman working in multiple male-dominated industries, such as residential painting, the construction trade, and the radio broadcasting business, I've learned that many times, men tend to treat women as:

1. They pretend they are not in the room.
2. The women are making too much noise.
3. They give them inappropriate, backhanded compliments.

When I founded **Sak Pase Media**, I began buying ads for others, including some of the men who had not supported me in the past. I had to make it clear that I expected to be treated with respect if they wished to work with me.

Another method I've employed to command respect is by controlling my reactions when faced with challenging situations. Women often face judgment and ridicule for displaying emotional or "dramatic" reactions and for embodying the "boss" persona. I have consistently made an effort to maintain my composure in public settings. I've read books and undergone training to become a better listener and control my emotional responses. This not only helps me present myself more effectively but has also improved my interviewing skills significantly.

It's unfortunately common for women to be perceived as talkative, which is sometimes unjustly viewed as a weakness. However, meaningful conversations are vital for building relationships, and we should be mindful of how we use our voices to create meaningful impacts.

Years ago, I participated in a Summit Education training that allowed me to explore new facets of myself. Later on, I joined Landmark training, where I identified unresolved issues that had been holding me back. By recognizing these obstacles, I could devise effective plans to overcome them. Throughout these training experiences, I learned that being a trainer also means being a lifelong learner, constantly seeking new ways to progress and avoid stagnation.

In the year 2000, prior to the aforementioned training experiences, I attended a Women's Issues and Diversity training hosted by the Professional Women Network in Louisville, KY. This training was a gift from my mother, who generously covered the expenses. It expanded my perspective on how each individual is unique yet interconnected in some way. It also helped me value my individuality and recognize that I am designed differently from others.

After completing this diversity training, I came to realize that my uniqueness is something to be celebrated and encouraged in others as well. I am the only child born to both my mother and father, which means I possess their exclusive DNA combination. Everyone has their own path, and I understand that I should refrain from making comparisons because God has crafted me to be unique.

The diversity training provided me with a fresh perspective on my mother and others, allowing me to comprehend their choices and appreciate them as distinct individuals. Listening to their stories has not only contributed to my personal growth but has also enabled me to become a better version of myself.

Women in business are often taken less seriously due to the multitude of roles and responsibilities they are expected to juggle. I have come to realize that my mother, along with many other women, always did their best. This realization has strengthened my relationship with my mother, and we now share a bond as two resilient women. I aspire to have a similar kind of relationship with my daughter, Natalie, as partners rather than just as mother and daughter.

Throughout my tenure as the host of the Koze Fanm show, I encountered several challenges that put my abilities to the test. In order to maintain a positive experience for my viewers, I had to adapt my demeanor and outlook.

I made a necessary adjustment that allowed me to continue hosting my show. I switched my schedule from broadcasting six days a week on a single station at 10:00 a.m. to 11:00 a.m. to broadcasting three days a week on multiple networks from 3:00 to 4:00 p.m. This change has been in effect since 2013 and allowed me to pursue other life plans while also becoming a syndicated radio talk show host. While these adjustments were not always easy, they provided me with enough time to focus on other areas of interest.

It's incredibly gratifying to know that the work you do is appreciated by other professionals in your field. However, don't wait for your dreams to manifest before you start making a difference. When I received the Best Communicator's Award from BOMA in 2017 for the Koze Fanm show, it held significant meaning for me, even though I didn't pursue it for fame. My goal then, as it is now, has always been to show up, do the work, and strive to connect and succeed.

A Woman's Professional Challenges

When I listen to the stories of phenomenal women like my mother Talina, my aunt Christiana, former First Lady of the United States Michelle Obama, Maya Angelou, Congresswoman Carrie Meek, Marleine Bastien, the Haitian singer Emeline Michel, Lucie Tondreau, and many others, I'm reminded that we all carry a mental image of ourselves. It's essential to ensure that this mental image is a positive one, as our intentions are good, and we never know who we might be inspiring to make positive changes in their lives.

As a woman, I often find myself with a surplus of ideas that I don't always get the chance to execute. We should strive to develop the habit of building confidence, assembling the right team, and finding the inner strength to stay motivated. It's crucial to practice habits that align with our values, bearing in mind that forming good habits takes time.

Taking care of our mental health and peace of mind is equally important, as is paying attention to our physical appearance and dressing in a manner that reflects how we wish to be addressed. That's an opportunity to help us grow and evolve to better serve. Visualizing the best version of ourselves and practicing the roles we currently occupy as our playground allows us to experiment with different approaches.

In our journey as women, what empowering beliefs can we adopt to help us achieve our goals? Let's refuse to be defeated by the challenges we encounter on the road of life. Cultivate the habit of being your own life coach and cheerleader, and summon the courage to trust and try again, no matter how many times it takes.

No matter what, self-control is an important skill to develop. Identify the triggers: the things, people, and situations that evoke certain feelings in you. Once you've pinpointed them, do your best to distance yourself from them. Finding an accountability partner really works. We shouldn't act like two-year-olds throwing tantrums to get our way. It's easy to feel like a victims of life's challenges. Recognize your self-worth, learn to manage your emotions, even when your needs aren't met yet, and take the time to analyze things. Lack of self-control can lead to various undesirable actions, such as anger, physical violence, or unhealthy coping mechanisms.

When we're feeling lonely, we must redirect our emotions towards the positive. As God's words say, 'I will never leave you nor forsake you. I am always with you.'

I envisioned a path to find meaning. When I launched my business in 2006, my plan was different from what unfolded in 2019. It was then that my business underwent a shift, aligning more with a phase in my life where I became more concerned about the legacy I would leave behind rather than what I could personally achieve.

I aspire to make a significant impact during my time on Earth. Before my time is up, I want to contribute to creating the world I envision for today's generation and those to come."

The professional world has historically been structured in a way that may have favored men's needs and perspectives, which has posed challenges for women striving to become leaders. Women often encounter obstacles that can either serve as opportunities for growth or as barriers to their progress. It's important to recognize that success and learning from mistakes are intertwined aspects of life. Sometimes, individuals may present opportunities that do not align with our moral or ethical principles, and in such cases, maintaining integrity is paramount, even if it means forgoing potential success. Remember, just because we are eager to succeed doesn't mean we have to compromise our values.

It is unfortunate that women frequently face a lack of respect and trust in their abilities, leading them to constantly strive to exceed expectations and struggle to earn second chances. Moreover, the issue of sexual harassment has persisted in the workplace for as long as I can recall, which is deeply concerning.

When I embarked on my radio career, I made a conscious effort to project a calm and amiable demeanor even when facing immense pressure. I felt the need to lower my energy level to avoid being perceived as aggressive, a stereotype that had been ingrained in me – the idea that some women may be seen as too pushy. However, it's crucial for women to assert themselves confidently, regardless of what others might think. True progress lies in breaking free from these stereotypes and challenging the biases that persist in the professional world.

As a woman in the media, facing challenges is inevitable. However, it's essential to recognize and celebrate the accomplishments of women of color who fearlessly make their mark in the media industry. Some of these remarkable women include Oprah Winfrey, Tamron Hall, Hoda Kotb, Whoopi Goldberg, Robin Roberts, Gayle King, Joy Reid, Abby Phillip, Stichiz, Jill Tracey, Tamara G, Yamiche Alcindor, Liliane Pierre-Paul, Rose P. C, Fany S., Tamara P., Elizabeth G, Dr. Flore, Djenane St-F, and many more.

During one of my hosting gigs, a male individual made a derogatory remark on the show, and I responded. He stated that I was "crazy" and should be disregarded. Despite this, I quickly stood up for myself and defended my character politely and thoughtfully to avoid offending my audience. When we endeavor to make a difference, some men attempt to label us as "crazy" or worse, questioning our integrity and ability to serve. One must wonder about the integrity of a man who had the audacity to insult me on my own show in front of a live audience.

Precile L was listening to the show when the guy made a peculiar comment, and she told me that I did the right thing by standing up for myself. It's crucial to take oneself seriously and act with grace. Always seek guidance from God for discernment. As a woman, I freely share my thoughts and sentiments, especially during tough times. I've learned the importance of expressing myself without needlessly offending others, especially when venting or expressing grievances.

Sometimes, people enjoy listening to our stories to draw comparisons. This concept ties back to a valuable lesson I learned from my mom. Since that particular experience, I've grown significantly in assertiveness, ensuring that I respect myself and others. I've embraced the role of a leader and entrepreneur, demanding respect from everyone I collaborate with. I see no alternative but to continue doing what's right with the utmost integrity and good intentions.

Throughout my career, I've witnessed shifts that have simplified matters and infused hope. An excellent example of this is the #MeToo movement, which has been a catalyst for significant change. As more women gather the courage to speak out, men are increasingly compelled to acknowledge our boundaries and treat them with respect.

Relatable

People who meet me often feel like they know me as a personal friend. They assume that I am transparent, even though there are aspects of my life I keep to myself. They believe they are connected to my happiness and my laughter. To me, the secret is not to forge situations but rather to allow yourself to be who you are and accept others as they are.

As women, we should thrive on making a difference and own up to who we are. We must keep our heads held high, regardless of our backgrounds. When we step into our power, we should let our light shine. Let's embrace the transformation as we evolve and grow toward our life's mission and purpose.

Reflection

"For I know the plans I have for you," declares the LORD, 'plans to prosper you and not to harm you, plans to give you hope and a future.' - Jeremiah 29:11 (NIV)

Journal Prompts

Go through the journey with hope and grace.

1. What are some women's issues that you have faced? How have you overcome them?
2. How have you worked to remove roadblocks for future women?
3. How are you shaping your legacy as a woman?
4. As a woman, where can you be more practical with your leadership?
5. What is your why, your goals, intentions, and purpose?

Tips to Adjust the Volume

- Don't be afraid to take action toward your mission and your calling.

- Get your mind right and quiet the noise to understand the message.

- Finding your voice is about understanding your message.

- Ask God to unseal your lips so that your words can be a source of blessing.

- Believe in yourself. When you are not sure, take an optimistic guess.

CHAPTER FIVE
Turning Adversity into Purpose

Psalms 32:8

The LORD says, "I will guide you along the best pathway for your life. I will advise you and watch over you.

Train yourself to find a reason to rise above any situation. You have the power to allow yourself to feel joy, laugh and smile again. Be thankful in advance, even when experiencing challenges; know that there's always more than meets the eye. Keep showing up, do your best to walk by faith and not by sight. Position yourself to allow positive energy to flow into your life. Blessings and lessons sometimes work together. You are never too old to learn. Give your all, every day and in every way, until you see the light. Today is a new day, and you have many reasons to be grateful. As difficult as things may seem, remember that we are our ancestors' answered prayers; let's not take our blessings and privileges for granted. We must have the courage to embrace the different seasons in our lives and remain hopeful for a brighter future.

The greatest moment of success is when you realize you came so close to quitting but didn't; that's the best way to extract blessings from life's lessons. There were times when I felt extremely unwell, yet that never deterred me from hosting the show. One day, I was in so much pain that I could barely leave the house, but I still made the decision to host the show, and strangely enough, once I started, I began to feel better.

If we were to depart from this world today, how would we be remembered? There is immense value in living life one moment at a time; the show taught me how to do just that. Many people are either overly concerned about tomorrow or stuck in the past. However, the present is the only moment we can truly influence and change. Often, we encounter numerous challenges that make us want to give up. From limitation to liberation, we must learn self-reliance. It involves developing the right attitude in every season of life, including self-control, avoiding negativity, staying open-minded, and working on acceptance. Smile more, whether in good or challenging times and maintain optimism while keeping your composure. Always be aware of God's presence in your life, regardless of the situation. Let your dreams and visions be the roadmap to your purpose. Every pain we experience brings new lessons into our lives if we pay attention to the present moment. Don't let doubt undermine God's promises. Lean not on your understanding; He has your back. Over the years, God has performed remarkable deeds in my life, and I praise Him for His greatness and blessings.

Life is a sequence of outcomes reflecting our inner dialogue; it's a manifestation of cause and effect. My mom always reminded me that we weren't all in the same boat, even though we may have weathered the same storm. This means our experiences and results are unique, so it's essential to choose what aligns with our own path.

Adversity often brings valuable experiences. If we approach it as a lesson, it can shape us into stronger individuals. Through adversity, we gain maturity, innovation, and resilience. As the famous saying goes, 'What doesn't kill you makes you stronger,' and learning to find joy even in hardship is a valuable skill.

We should be mindful of what we allow into our minds and personal space, as some things in life are irreversible. Remember that everything happens for a reason, and disappointments and closed doors have the power to shape us into who we are today. Women face unique challenges, including confidence, hormonal changes, and body image issues, which can affect their emotions and perspectives. It's crucial to stay adaptable during these ups and downs and to train our minds to be more resilient than our emotions.

Take note of your accomplishments and appreciate the journey. Your actions in defining moments can either build or break you. Don't gamble with your life, as your destiny is on the line.

Challenging moments are an inevitable part of life, but they are not permanent. Regardless of the gravity of our difficulties, it's essential to give ourselves a chance to heal and gain an understanding of the circumstances.

It may appear challenging to navigate certain situations or maintain the status quo, but in due time, your reality can exceed your wildest dreams. Recognizing that your goals may evolve and change over time is essential. To embrace change and adjust to the new normal, it's vital to position yourself accordingly and prepare to thrive in new ways.

Keeping an open mind and considering new approaches is crucial. Instead of waiting for circumstances to improve, we can shift our perspective to find happiness in the present moment, avoiding potential regrets. By retraining ourselves to adapt to different situations, we can eventually discover the best path forward.

Seizing the energy and making the most of the present moment is essential in preparing for the unpredictable twists and turns of our complex and interconnected world. We should strive to have a positive impact on our lives and the lives of others, leaving a lasting legacy. Remember, closed doors can often lead to better opportunities, so have faith in the unknown future and keep moving forward.

Our experiences, whether good or bad, contribute to new ways of understanding. Through these experiences, we develop a fresh vision and become more receptive to better possibilities. However, it's easier to grasp this when we know what we're dealing with. When we're dissatisfied with the outcomes, it's essential to figure out how to move forward and break free from stagnation.

The year 2020 marked an unprecedented time for all of us due to the COVID-19 pandemic. Our daily routines came to a halt as the world implemented measures to slow the virus's spread. Some believed the situation would resolve within a few weeks, and life would return to normal. However, that wasn't the case.

I made a conscious effort to safeguard my mental health by limiting my exposure to the pandemic's tragic impact on the world. Instead, I focused on what truly matters—my personal growth, spiritual life, and my relationship with myself.

The periods of lockdown and social distancing were undeniably challenging. Yet, they provided us with an opportunity to rediscover and appreciate things we had previously taken for granted. I viewed it as a chance to find harmony within myself. Now, several years have passed, and we are still grappling with the pandemic. Eventually, the pandemic may subside or become a part of history. However, who we have become during this crisis will remain with us forever.

The years 2018 and 2019 marked the beginning of a season of change in my life. Regardless of how challenging it felt, I prefer to view it as a period of 'mindfulness.'

Like many others, I faced numerous difficulties in 2020. However, those struggles were essentially an extension of a major hardship I experienced in early 2019—the loss of my mother. Despite these challenging times, I gained valuable insights into God's grace and mercy, discovered the boundless reservoirs of strength within me, and deepened my understanding of the workings of life itself. Through this prolonged struggle, I learned many valuable lessons and ultimately emerged victorious.

It's essential to maintain optimism and have faith in yourself. Remember that combining faith with action can lead to miraculous outcomes."

James 2:14-17

14 What good is it, my brothers and sisters, if someone claims to have faith but has no deeds? Can such faith save them? 15 Suppose a brother or a sister is without clothes and daily food. 16 If one of you says to them, "Go in peace; keep warm and well fed," but does nothing about their physical needs, what good is it? 17 In the same way, faith by itself, if it is not accompanied by action, is dead.

Here are the lessons I learned during this time:

I am so grateful to God for placing me on my path.

Be on the quest for personal transformation and self-improvement projects. Start working on yourself to evolve. Your willingness to make an impact in the lives of the people you come in contact with by using your knowledge and ability can start creating new ways to help and assist others in seeing the light, and from there, new opportunities will arise to improve your life and your income.

Every day is a new opportunity to grow.

- We can breathe through it, smile, and still count our blessings.
- It was an opportunity for a digital transformation.
- It was an opportunity to re-evaluate my assets, keep what's working, and let go of what's not.
- God has no plans to abandon us.

As I mentioned earlier, I became a Medicare insurance representative in 2018. This new experience brought me closer to the older generation and taught me to appreciate the struggles of elders from different cultures. Then, in 2019, I unexpectedly lost my mother, Talina. She was a significant figure in my life, serving as both my friend and role model. She played a major role in shaping me into the woman I am today. I was unprepared for her death, and it plunged me into a deep depression that lasted for months.

When she passed away, the timing didn't feel right. I yearned for more time with my mom. However, less than a year later, when the world shut down due to COVID-19, I found myself profoundly grateful for God's timing. If she had passed during the pandemic, my children and I probably wouldn't have been able to travel to Haiti to pay our respects at her funeral. Additionally, she might not have been able to have the funeral she deserved due to the political unrest in Haiti.

Now that I'm more mature, I prioritize my peace and joy. It's fulfilling to witness my manifestations turning into reality, all while knowing that God is alongside me in every battle. I've navigated through various types of pain, including family issues, trust concerns, insecurities, heartbreaks, and more. Throughout it all, I not only survived but thrived, and this resilience is rooted in my unwavering faith in God.

I have confidence that my God possesses insider knowledge, and this trust fuels my belief in victory awaiting on the other side of every challenge. Cultivating a lifestyle centered on gratitude has become a top priority for me. Ultimately, life is about the obstacles we conquer, not just the accomplishments we attain.

Even though these past two years have been challenging, I've emerged stronger, and this transformation wouldn't have been possible without the hard work and self-help I invested in along the way.

The Call of Reasoning

On Tuesday, April 23, 2019, as I was en route to the studio to host the Koze Fanm show, my mom called. She spoke with a grave tone and said, "Listen to me, Guylene, I have something very important to tell you." I will never forget that day; it marked the last time I spoke with my mother. Our conversation had a profound impact on my life, one that I'll cherish forever. Sometimes, I attempt to replay it, but I've come to realize that nothing is more valuable than the present moment. I believe she sensed that her time was drawing near, prompting her to make the call. She had her household helper rush to the store to purchase a calling card and ask him for some privacy to talk to me.

I needed to attend a brief meeting before the show, and just as I was about to enter the meeting room, my mother called again. I was in such a rush that day that I couldn't disconnect the call, as my mom had paid for that long-distance call. I entered the meeting while keeping my mother on the line, half-listening as I hurriedly attended to business matters before heading to the station to host the show. Even with only half of my attention, that conversation compelled me to take my life more seriously and focus on what truly matters. I refer to it as "the call of the journey."

Despite being 46 years old at the time, she told me, "You're nearly 50, and it's time for you to start taking things more seriously and assume greater responsibility in various aspects of your life."

She was granting me permission to embrace my responsibilities as a woman, mother, daughter, and human being. She wanted me to step into my role as a queen.

She said, "Stop dedicating all your time to helping others and neglecting yourself. It's admirable to assist people, but now it's time to take charge of what you already have and make it work. As you grow older, your years of working as hard as you do now are limited. With your children now grown, it's time for you to focus on your future and secure your retirement. Don't take things for granted. Open your eyes and see what lies ahead."

My mother always used to tell me, "Mete Fanm sou ou pou'w kapab regle zafè'w, tande," which in Creole means "Rise up as a woman so you can handle your affairs." This call served as a powerful reminder to do just that.

During our conversation, she also urged me to draw closer to God and strengthen my relationship with Him. She emphasized not underestimating my investments and provided me with crucial information to help me move forward.

I believe my mother knew this would be our final conversation. It's as if she sensed it would be our last earthly exchange. I suspect she had more to share, but our call was abruptly cut short. Rather than immediately calling her back, I assumed we could continue our conversation on Sunday, our usual day to talk.

Regrettably, my mother passed away that very Sunday between 5:00 and 6:00 a.m. We never had the chance to conclude our last discussion.

For the following several months, I carried an overwhelming burden of guilt. I was not only deeply saddened by my mother's passing, but I also wrestled with remorse for not being by her side in Haiti. I felt anger at the lack of communication regarding the severity of her declining health or any encouragement to call her more frequently. These emotions dragged me into the darkest place I had ever experienced. The woman who had been my friend, counselor, and mentor was no longer there to guide me through the pain of her loss.

Several months later, I recollected that final conversation, which granted me strength and pulled me out of the abyss. I learned to lean on my relationship with God, relying on Him during my most challenging moments. I clung to my mother's words, urging me to 'woman up,' and I persevered. I worked to find inner peace, seeking God's assistance. I realized that I must constantly adjust the volume to allow peace to shine brighter than the pain."

This experience taught me a crucial lesson: When you have a message, you must deliver it. That's exactly what my mom did when she called me. You can't afford to wait to share your feelings and passions. Thanks to my mother's example, I now feel more confident, bold, and liberated to express my message and live life to the fullest. I believe she granted me both permission and strength to embrace my true self.

That final conversation with my mom completely transformed my life and my perspective. It compelled me to embrace my responsibilities and search for the silver lining in every situation, even when the circumstances appeared unfavorable at the time. It was like assembling a scattered puzzle board, where all the pieces were there, but this conversation helped me see how they fit together perfectly, creating a beautiful picture.

This call also influenced how I approach relationships, as I've learned to prioritize safeguarding my peace of mind and expecting the same from others. This shift has replaced a significant void with self-love and has led to more positive outcomes.

Whenever I need strength, I revisit this conversation and others we've had in the past. My mom was preparing me to excel independently. I remember the time she told me, "You must open your eyes. It's essential to protect your interests and prioritize what matters most to you. You need to be discerning about who you allow into your inner circle."

She raised me to be a strong woman, equipping me for a life without her. One of the most cherished compliments she ever bestowed upon me was, "You always seek your own path, and you're unafraid to dance alone."

At that time, I didn't fully comprehend it, but she was nurturing my ability to rely on my inner strength and the grace of God, enabling me to embrace my true self and all the potential within me. The trials and tribulations I encountered provided me with the courage I required to progress and flourish. I thank God for His favor in guiding me through all of life's challenges.

Rest, reset, Recharge

Learn to prioritize your self-worth and grant yourself the right to recharge. Cultivate self-compassion and self-acceptance as a means to rejuvenate your energy. Everything can feel overwhelming when exhaustion sets in, be it physical or emotional. Grief and uncertainty can be particularly draining, which is why it's crucial to offer ourselves the kindness to rest during challenging periods.

Striving for inner peace and a healthier version of yourself is a responsibility that you owe to yourself.

There are many benefits to rest, including:

Find ways to:

- Reduced stress and anxiety
- Decreased blood pressure
- Chronic pain relief

- Improved immune health
- Improved mood

Our quality sleep can help us rest, recover, and recharge. While I was going through the turmoil of losing my mom, I spent a lot of sleepless nights trying to understand and deal with different kinds of feelings and emotions. I realized that the less I slept, the more it affected my emotional and physical state. So, I asked myself, "How can you better prioritize rest and sleep?"

Although I am still working on it, here are some of the things that work for me:

- Listening to music
- Reading a book
- Taking a bath
- Avoiding caffeine in the afternoon and evening
- Making sure I'm not hungry/ hydration
- Drinking tea
- Praying
- A combination of these things may work

After my mother passed away, it was time for me to take charge and learn how to handle things on my own. The endless source of wisdom I had once relied upon was no longer available, so I had to figure things out for myself and my children.

By 2020, I had finally found peace after my mother's death. However, the world was about to be shaken in a way that none of us could have expected. The coronavirus swept across the Earth and left everyone in a state of panic. Most of the world went into a relatively strict lockdown for several months, and for over a year, we experienced a new normal.

The lockdowns that began in the middle of March 2020 were highly unusual. It felt as if we were preparing for an apocalypse. Schools closed down, travel was restricted, and many people were instructed to work from home. Job losses were rampant, and people felt uncertain and adrift.

As humans, we often keep going until we exhaust ourselves and experience burnout. We work ourselves to a point where we quit because we become too overwhelmed to function. Despite the internal turmoil that many people experienced, the world slowed down. There were very few cars on the streets, and airplanes were scarce in the skies. It became eerily quiet, and we were forced to rest.

People who used to be occupied with work, social events, kids' extracurricular activities, and the chaos of daily life suddenly found themselves with time to spend at home. Family dinners became a regular occurrence, people picked up new hobbies, and we learned to relax. Our society had become so busy, but during the lockdowns, we were compelled to take a break and rest physically.

This is not to say that the situation was all rainbows and butterflies; it was not. It was incredibly challenging. However, it served as a stark reminder that we need to rest, not quit, when we become weary.

I have come to realize that I need to be intentional about slowing down and allowing myself to rest. I can't afford to wait until a crisis forces me to come to a halt. I must be mature enough to recognize when I need a break. Remember that resting is a crucial component of our overall health and self-care, and we all need to prioritize it.

Find Your Frequency And Adjusting Your Emotional Volume.

At some point in your life, when you realize that no one is coming to save you, dare to tap into your infinite source and become your own superhero. Taking the time to reconnect with ourselves is the key to translating our dreams into action. Too often, we become lost because we are out of touch with ourselves. Overcoming grief requires healing and transformation. It's important to recognize that moving on from a situation that no longer serves our purpose is perfectly acceptable. Pay attention and understand yourself well enough to avoid situations that tend to draw you back to places you've struggled to move away from.

Sometimes, you need to distance yourself without explanation. You have nothing to prove to anyone. As we approach the future, we'll discover new ways to find sunshine through the clouds and shed our masks.

Between losing my mother and the pandemic, I've learned the importance of adjusting my emotional response. These challenges can overwhelm you if you don't manage your emotions effectively.

One of the best ways to regulate your emotional responses is to take stock of your feelings and be mindful of your thoughts and emotions when you're troubled. To do this, allocate some dedicated time for yourself. This is a practice my mom instilled in me from a young age. She used to wake up early in the morning to enjoy a cup of coffee before anyone else was up. It provided her with an opportunity to reflect on her actions from the previous day and plan for a better today and a brighter future."

Taking this time for yourself enables you to make corrections and improvements, granting you the ability to envision your future.

As previously mentioned, my mother's passing plunged me into a dark place, and depression consumed my life. About three months after her death, I prayed earnestly, expressing to God my inability to continue due to the overwhelming pain. This moment of prayer prompted me to recognize the need to adjust my feelings, mindset, and perspective on the pain I was experiencing. I had to muster the courage to persevere.

Praying to God is one effective way to allocate that necessary time for reflection. I turned to prayer to address my depression because I was reluctant to rely on medication. Around mid-July 2019, I had a significant dream. In the dream, my mother appeared and asked me to make room for her to lie beside me. Since that dream, I've felt as though she gave me the strength to press on.

I encourage individuals to discover their favorite Bible verse, words of affirmation, or music that can serve as a remote control to adjust the volume of negative thoughts in their minds. Do not allow negative thoughts to linger; you must learn to locate and regulate your mental and emotional dial. Here are a few methods to help you find and manage that dial:

- Think of a time when you have successfully and intentionally changed your thoughts to move forward. How did you do this? Can you do it again?
- Acknowledge your emotions. Where are you, and where do you want to be?
- Listen to good music. Tune in to what makes you happy.
- Find a support system that you can rely on.
- Know that you are not alone, and God is always with you through tough times.
- Take a look at your recovery process. How can it be tweaked to be more effective?

If you are dealing with a specific loss, whether it's the loss of a loved one, a relationship, or a job, it's crucial to take time to grieve. Understand that the feelings associated with such losses may never completely vanish, but you must confront them to move forward. Identify which emotions are linked to guilt and address them appropriately.

Determine strategies for managing your mental health and establishing your priorities. Recognize when it's necessary to prioritize yourself and when to say "no." You don't have to answer every call or pursue every opportunity.

Even as you navigate emotional pain, remember to take care of your physical well-being. Don't forget to eat, sleep, drink water, and engage in physical activities that bring you joy.

In hindsight, I am grateful for God's blessings. Despite all the challenges I've faced, I have persevered. Keeping this in mind allows me to continue dreaming and stay on course, regardless of any fear, worry, or doubt.

During that period in my life, it was challenging to fully appreciate living in the moment. I had to make adjustments to overcome doubts, distractions, and the negative inner voice to connect better with myself and those around me. I realized that by applying the same techniques in other aspects of my life, I could make progress.

Don't take it personally

Learn to control yourself and how you react, both in public and in private. Another valuable lesson I picked up during the 2018-2020 era is the importance of not taking things too personally. No matter what "it" is, over-analyzing it will weigh you down and negatively impact your decision-making. I don't always try to understand everything or everyone for the sake of my peace of mind and sanity. You have to accept that people don't do things because of you; they do them because they want to. When you learn to separate yourself from the actions of others, you won't feel attacked. Taking things personally will not only harm you but also damage your relationships.

Think about a situation where you're in a conflict with someone you care about. Things can get heated, and people may say things they don't actually mean. If you internalize those words, it can harm both you and your relationships.

Sometimes, we misinterpret things, so taking them personally can be harmful, especially if the person didn't mean what we thought they did. Taking things personally can also prevent us from thinking things through.

As a teenager, I once got angry with one of my sisters over something she did. We were experiencing sibling rivalry, so I reported her behavior to our mom. My mom listened quietly to everything I had to say. The quieter she remained about the situation, the more I kept talking, bringing up things that had happened before. Eventually, she grew tired of listening.

She looked at me with a side-eye and said, "Is that all you have to say?" Then she got up and remarked, "You had a lot to share with me, my daughter. Pray for wisdom, okay?" Afterward, she walked away. That didn't alleviate my frustration at the moment. However, as I grew older, I came to realize a few things about that conversation that made me more aware of my attitude.

It made me realize how crucial self-control is from a very young age. Back then, I was heavily involved in church work, and I had to introspect and question whether my attitude reflected the teachings of God. Additionally, I learned that we should never make significant decisions when we are upset, tired, or confused. It's essential to be mindful of your emotions when facing important choices, as positive emotions can help overcome negative ones.

Before we can lead others, we must learn to lead ourselves. This means practicing self-awareness, self-confidence, and self-efficiency. We also need to be willing to address unwanted emotions. It was a chance for me to make some changes as a child of God. I needed to pray for wisdom. After all, my sisters are family, and it's crucial to have each other's backs.

Furthermore, it's essential to recognize that people are inherently different from us. In our world, we encounter individuals from diverse cultures and linguistic backgrounds, which can influence how we interpret their words and actions. Language and cultural barriers can become obstacles if we fail to consider them. However, embracing these differences can lead to personal growth and foster diversity and inclusion. Varied communication styles can sometimes create challenges in both personal and professional relationships.

It's vital to grasp that living as a child of God can provide protection in various situations. What makes taking things personally dangerous is that it can lead us to internalize criticism. It's crucial to understand the source of criticism and discern whether it stems from a place of love or hatred. This discernment can help us respond more effectively and maintain our inner peace.

Connecting with Others

Let's take the time to discover God's presence within ourselves before we seek to connect with others. In that discovery, we find wisdom, knowledge, and power.

I had to adapt my networking approach during the COVID-related lockdowns, as in-person meetings became impossible. Consequently, mastering the art of networking through technology has become increasingly important. I utilize social media and the phone to establish connections. I've also redirected my attention to platforms I had previously resisted, including Facebook, YouTube, and Instagram. I've made a concerted effort to share uplifting messages and acknowledge individuals who are making positive contributions both on my radio show, on social media, and in person.

One noteworthy initiative I embarked upon during the pandemic was speaking at a Zoom web conference. I discussed the effective use of social media groups for communication. Many people misuse Facebook groups, violating their policies, but when utilized correctly, they can be a valuable resource. Thus, I also addressed the importance of proper communication on social media.

Additionally, I had the opportunity to speak about maintaining our resolve and not allowing negativity to infiltrate our minds. This topic held particular significance for me because I firmly believe that a positive mindset is the foundation of both success and happiness."

Lessons from Being a Media Host

"My experience in radio has been invaluable during this challenging period. The lessons I've gathered from over a decade on the air have proven to be incredibly useful. Through this journey, I've grown, gained a deeper understanding of myself, and come to realize my worth as a constantly evolving individual. Over the years, I've celebrated numerous victories, each one a testament to the blessings, training, and lessons that have shaped me as I continue to pursue my dreams. It has been placed upon my heart to help others in various ways, to help them truly come alive.

When I first ventured into daytime radio, it was predominantly a male-dominated space. I encountered several instances where listeners, mostly men, would call into my show and make disparaging remarks. They seemed uncomfortable with a woman's voice in the radio realm. Given that "Koze Fanm" means "women's issues," some assumed I was a feminist, expecting my show to be inherently anti-men. However, this was far from the truth. As they realized that I remained dedicated to my vision of empowering the Haitian community by providing opportunities and resources, they began to respect me and appreciate what I brought to the airwaves.

I am profoundly grateful to God for safeguarding and guiding me throughout this journey. The Bible teaches us that faith doesn't necessarily make things easy, but it does make them possible.

With His wisdom and guidance, I have been able to pull many lessons from these experiences. Here are a few specific things that helped me:

1. Taking time to examine my life

2. Remembering to live in the moment

3. Inviting God to assist me, always

4. Being grateful for the things that give me joy and counting my blessings

5. Slowing down to take time to appreciate things that I usually speed by

6. Embracing the things that could make a shift in my mood in a positive way

7. Identifying "quick fixes" for mood enhancement (such as music, food, and conversation with someone with positive energy or a walk/drive by the beach).

8. Paying less attention to things that don't work and focus on what does work so I can do more of what gives me a burst of laughter, joy, or fulfillment.

9. Reflecting on life with a sense of praise and gratefulness

10. Realizing that how I show up for myself has a lot to do with how I show up in the world

"The show has imparted invaluable lessons in discipline, structure, intentionality, and purposefulness to me. It has helped me cultivate flexibility in my thinking and a genuine appreciation for spontaneity. I've come to understand that when one door closes, often, another one opens, and sometimes, the new one is even better. I firmly believe that by consistently moving forward, I will eventually encounter success.

I've also learned the importance of resilience in achieving goals. Whether it's dealing with a painful breakup, a divorce, the loss of a loved one, a setback in business, or betrayal from friends, holding onto pain and resentment only obstructs progress. It's crucial to gain a clear perspective on life, let go of the past, and wholeheartedly embrace the future.

In life, it's essential to remain open, adaptable, and prepared for change. There are moments when you must contain the flame, and there are moments when you must ignite it. Understanding yourself and your desires will help you discern the appropriate course of action.

Reader Reflection

"Be strong and courageous. Do not be afraid or terrified because of them, for the Lord your God goes with you; he will never leave you nor forsake you." - Deuteronomy 31:6 (NIV)

"So do not fear, for I am with you; do not be dismayed, for I am your God. I will strengthen you and help you; I will uphold you with my righteous right hand." - Isaiah 41:10 (NIV)

Journal Prompts

Think of a difficult situation and answer these questions:

1. What's the lesson in this?
2. What's possible now?
3. Who else can I help?

Here are some of the positive affirmations that have helped me stay encouraged throughout the years:

1. I am healthy.

2. I am willing to change and grow.

3. My past is not a reflection of my future.

4. I am strong enough to make my own decisions.

5. I'm in control of how I react to others.

6. I'm choosing peace.

7. I am wise.

8. I'm courageous and stand up for myself.

9. I believe that with God, all things are possible.

10. I can succeed.

11. I am fearfully and beautifully made.

12. I deserve to feel joy.

13. I am in alignment with my mind, body, and spirit.

14. I can love and be loved.

15. I love myself deeply.

16. My body is healthy, and I'm grateful.

17. I'm more at ease every day.

18. I believe that all things work together for good.

19. I'm calm, happy, and content.

20. My life is a gift, and I appreciate everything I have.

21. I am prosperous.

22. I surround myself with positive people who will help bring out the best in me.

23. I don't need someone else to make me feel happy.

24. I choose to balance harmony and peace in my life.

25. My life is beautiful.

Tips to Adjust the Volume

- Live your best life.
- Write your own life story.
- Don't seek validation.
- Dress like you would want to be addressed.
- Be kind to yourself.
- Make yourself a priority.
- Protect your emotions.
- Allow God to work in your life.

CHAPTER SIX
Relationships and Self-Discovery

Life is about relationships; nurture the good ones, starting with yourself. If you want a soul mate, take time to heal your soul. When engaging in a relationship, it's essential to remember that building trust takes time. Cultivating the right relationships throughout your lifetime is the best way to enjoy a fulfilling life. However, a genuine connection starts from within. So, learn to understand yourself and tap into the infinite power and wisdom within you. Be mindful of the stories you tell yourself, tame your ego, and be open to transformation. Become more aware of what brings you joy, examine yourself, discover your triggers, and make adjustments accordingly. We have much to learn on this journey through the people we encounter, meet, live with, and network with.

It's important to make a habit of regularly recognizing and appreciating the small joys in our lives. Feeling valued, protected, and safe is crucial in any relationship. We should prioritize self-love and leave any situation that doesn't honor our dignity and personal boundaries. Embrace your unique journey towards self-appreciation to achieve a happier life. Surround yourself with positive energies that can help you heal from past experiences and allow yourself to grow beyond any pain, envisioning a brighter future.

I've learned that we become entwined in the way people express love, and that shapes our relationships. It's more important how we perceive the world than how the world perceives us. Let's remain mindful of our expectations, perspectives, and assumptions to lead a more fulfilling life. Have you ever wondered what you truly desire and value in a relationship? Relationships involve the sharing and nurturing of intimacy, which entails revealing our vulnerabilities and values.

Our relationships play a significant role in our lives, and it's important to appreciate both the time spent alone and with others. While some relationships can be enriching, others may not be as healthy. It's crucial to refrain from excessively criticizing our family members, as hurt and guilt are inevitable aspects of life. Nevertheless, learning how to forgive and mend relationships to move forward is equally important. Although our choices can be challenging, seeking liberation can be a profoundly freeing experience. Today, strive to find ways to invite positivity into your life.

1. The state of being related or interrelated

2. The relation connecting or binding participants in a relationship

3. A form of affairs existing between those having relations or dealings

With those definitions in mind, there are two rules to keep in mind for all types of relationships:

1. People flourish by encouragement.
2. Repeat rule number one.
3. Practice the law of reciprocity.

I encourage you to explore and get to know yourself before engaging in any serious relationship. Know your worth and take inventory of yourself before you ask someone to invest their love, energy, and attention in you.

When it comes to communication, we can convey more by staying silent. It's important to be mindful that everyone has something happening behind the scenes, even if they are putting on a smile for the camera. Be generous and share your smile often, even if it's with a stranger.

In my younger years, my mom encouraged me to pray for humility, and my dad taught me to pray for discernment. As I've grown older, this advice has proven invaluable, especially in determining which relationships are worth pursuing. It has allowed me to radiate a sense of peace and contribute to healthy relationships. Relying on God's guidance when faced with choices between right and wrong has been particularly helpful. Life experiences have also illuminated the wisdom behind my parents' teachings.

What Do We Want in a Relationship?

As I mentioned earlier, each relationship is unique because each serves a different purpose. For example, your relationship with your sibling will be vastly different from your relationship with your spouse. However, communication is the key to success in any relationship. What we hear and say can be a source of nourishment for the relationship. We must be more mindful and attuned to each other's emotions.

While relationships may seem natural, they require effort to establish and maintain. This applies to relationships of any nature, whether they are romantic, familial, or professional.

Before embarking on a new relationship, it is crucial to understand what you desire from that relationship. Without this understanding, it's challenging to build a relationship on a solid foundation. Discovering your needs in a relationship is a deeply personal process. It necessitates reflection and introspection to understand your intentions. Additionally, you should put in equal effort to learn and comprehend each other's mutual needs and emotions.

Remember that a healthy relationship consists of shared emotions, mutual caring, a keen understanding, the ability to relate, and good communication. It is crucial to communicate to eliminate assumptions. Part of healthy communication is regulating your emotions to control your response to events within the relationship. It's best to remain calm and composed when handling important matters to be more effective. Make sure you stay level-headed when facing major issues or making decisions. Respect yourself, set boundaries, and stay committed, but it's also okay to prioritize your own needs and desires. As you grow and change, make sure to communicate your personal growth to your partner. With age and experience, you'll become more skilled at navigating different relationships and supporting your loved ones. Remember that personal development is beneficial for the health of the relationship. You can foster a happier and healthier connection with your partner by cultivating a positive mindset and nurturing the relationship.

Here are a few questions to ask yourself to help you define your version of a healthy relationship:

- Is the other person aware of my needs?
- Am I honoring the other person's needs?
- What new things can I do to make the relationship better?
- What am I looking for in the relationship?
- What are the deal breakers for me in the relationship?

Make sure you assess your relationships regularly to maintain a positive inner circle.

Appreciation in Relationships

Show your appreciation; it may cost you nothing, but it means a lot. Would you rather be loved or respected? To me, both are important. The key to a successful relationship is appreciation. Appreciation opens the door to receiving more love, happiness, and compassion.

Relationships are essential in every aspect of life. However, your relationship with yourself is the most rewarding thing in life and the foundation of everything else. The different stages in my life taught me various things about relationships. When I was a young girl, I dreamed of how my prince would come and sweep me off my feet one day. He would love me, marry me, and one day, we'd have children.

I got married at 21 years old. We had two babies fairly quickly, and the situation became tough as we tried to get to know each other while facing unemployment, among other challenges. The relationship was filled with broken pieces and challenges. Eventually, we got divorced after 12 years of marriage, and I became a single mother to my two beautiful children. I am very grateful for a few people in my life who were there to support and love me unconditionally.

Even if you can't see a clear path now, I want to remind you that God has an amazing plan for your life. There is a reason you've made it this far. We must understand that some people are only meant to be part of a chapter, and sometimes, we must summon the courage to turn the page.

As I approached my 40s, I desired to be in a committed relationship. I was concerned that being a 40-year-old woman might make it difficult to attract a partner, so I began dating someone. In the beginning, it was beautiful; however, over time, he became increasingly controlling and used manipulation tactics to assert his dominance in the relationship. He seemed to have a need to feel superior, not just to me but to others as well. Well, that relationship didn't last long.

Sometimes, we might feel compelled to stay in a relationship just for the sake of having someone and because they make promises that they've got our back. During such times, we may overlook the imperfections in the relationship and even justify them. However, it's essential to remain true to our self-love and not compromise our personal values. We should also be vigilant about any changes within ourselves, even if our partner claims to love us. Sometimes, people may attempt to bind and control us under the guise of love.

The most significant lesson from this situation is that, regardless of how much someone professes their love for you, it's essential to pay attention to their actions. Possession does not equal love. Be vigilant and open your heart to truly listen. Trust your intuition to discern the necessary actions for self-preservation. Even in a relationship, you are still on a journey of self-discovery. Embrace your individuality. Know your desires and what brings you happiness.

Someone once told me, 'In a dark place, we find ourselves, and a little more knowledge lights our way,' a quote by Yoda, the Jedi master in Star Wars. Seek the purpose behind your pain. As we evolve, we all experience different stages and transformations in our lives. Find the courage to stand up for what matters to you.

Reflecting on my past, I rediscovered life and myself in my 40s. I am grateful for my strength in navigating difficult situations and for the valuable lessons that contributed to my personal growth. It would have been easy to fall into a cycle that could have robbed me of joy, freedom, values, and, potentially, even my life. We must learn to love ourselves, foster confidence, and discover our purpose to take action and enjoy the life we desire.

Over the years, I have learned that moving on is acceptable, starting anew is acceptable, and saying no is perfectly fine. However, enduring a situation where you don't feel valued, appreciated, or happy should not be tolerated. Love should not be draining or controlling, leaving you feeling stressed, inferior, depleted, depressed, or lost. Real love nurtures and brings out the best in you. As I began to love myself, my relationships with everyone around me also underwent a transformation.

Good relationships are essential for a business owner. The people in your life can either make or break you. In the radio business, as well as in my other entrepreneurial endeavors, taking the time to build relationships and understanding that everybody has something going on in their lives has been incredibly important. Whether it's my advertisers, sponsors, listeners, or even my competitors, finding a way to relate to others is crucial. I've made an effort to understand people's goals and motivations to help build deeper connections. This creates more sustainable and genuine relationships. Additionally, simply being kind can take you a long way.

The purpose of building these relationships and sowing seeds is to create a strong, reliable network. You never know when you might need someone else's services or expertise, and you never know when you may need to call on the help of a mutual acquaintance. By nurturing these relationships, you can tap into others as a resource and be a resource to others as well.

This is all easier said than done. Although I've made it a point to create opportunities and open doors for others, I've encountered significant resistance. I genuinely wanted to help others grow, but it's common for people to reinforce the barriers of competition rather than accepting invitations for collaboration. I've seen many people opt to work independently rather than join forces with me.

However, as the captain of your ship, you must remain vigilant and alert, for even a small hole can sink a large vessel. It's essential to be mindful of your mental health and prioritize its protection at all costs. If someone is not eager to collaborate, it's often better to part ways with them. It could be seen as a form of divine protection, preventing you from encountering a negative experience. Moving on demonstrates your power to safeguard the ship and keep it from sinking.

Communication in Relationships

Communication plays a vital role in any relationship. Fortunately, I have acquired a great deal of knowledge about relationships through life experiences, training, and work in broadcasting. Communication isn't just about speaking; it's also an opportunity to practice the art of listening. Body language and silence are equally vital elements. It's essential to discern which statements require a verbal response and which are best answered with silence and to know the appropriate responses for different situations. These techniques are practical in any relationship.

To enhance my listening skills, I found it necessary to practice concentration and mind-body connection. With numerous responsibilities in my life, it's easy to become distracted and lose focus. However, as an interviewer for my show, it was crucial for me to develop strong listening skills. To achieve this, I consciously prioritized the ongoing conversation and remained fully engaged with my guests. I also learned to control my reactions, a skill that has proven beneficial in my personal relationships as well.

Improving my feedback skills has further enhanced my communication abilities, both on the radio and in my personal relationships. It's crucial to pause before reacting or responding to someone. Taking time to reflect alters how I reply or react to others. When I fully absorb their thoughts, my immediate responses tend to be more constructive and thoughtful.

Based on my past experiences as an interpreter, I've learned that eliminating distractions is crucial for understanding conversations amidst noise. This skill has helped me pinpoint where to focus my attention and grasp the main points effectively.

Sometimes, seeking clarification is necessary, and it's perfectly acceptable to ask for it. It's valuable to maintain active listening because you never know what you'll learn, even when hearing a story several times.

During my formative years, my mom often repeated the same stories. This repetition didn't bother me because I gleaned something new each time, realizing that mood plays a pivotal role in storytelling. Listening multiple times can yield fresh insights, much like how a river never flows through the same spot twice. The same holds true for a story or lesson.

Expressing genuine interest in what someone is sharing helps them open up more, fostering a more authentic conversation. This is a principle I've also observed in coaching and training. By actively listening to someone, you create a space for them to discover their own solutions.

In communication, when you're listening, it's important to consider everything that is shared—both inputs and outputs. In other words, what you say and what you listen to are equally significant. Additionally, it's crucial to remember that confidence cannot replace preparation; however, it is essential for developing your communication skills.

As we grow older, we must learn to respond in a way that minimizes drama and carefully assesses our responsibilities. Engaging in some introspection can help us determine the best time and approach to resolving conflicts in our lives as promptly as possible.

We can always use our past experiences to learn from and gain a better understanding of the present, allowing us to handle it with confidence. Pay close attention to your body language, tone of voice, and the words you use. Be mindful of what you say to others because shame and guilt can severely damage relationships.

Regardless of the type of relationship, never underestimate the power of communication. A simple good morning text, a compliment, or even an apology can make a significant difference.

Understanding How We Got Here

Having a clear understanding of our purpose is essential for achieving personal success. Failure should be viewed as a stepping stone toward our goals, and we must strive to find ways to make things work. As someone passionate about gathering new ideas, I've found great success in my career in radio. While I may not have amassed millions or billions, it has allowed me to establish valuable connections and relationships.

Hosting a radio talk show provided me with valuable access to the community, and I am grateful for the opportunity it afforded me. Thanks to the show, I've had the chance to meet numerous individuals whom I may not have crossed paths with otherwise.

Being a media host opened doors for me to connect with leaders and stakeholders in the community. Some became great partners, while others became dear friends. Either way, we've supported each other on our respective journeys. I even had the privilege of meeting lawmakers from the US at the Capitol, and I had an encounter with President Barack Obama. I became a media strategist for political candidates, governmental agencies, and corporations. This experience helped me develop confidence, find my voice, and continue pursuing my true purpose while also educating and informing myself to better serve my community.

"Radio has served as the foundation for my experiences and connections, providing me with the courage to pursue my passions.

I have a strong belief in the power and value of relationships, to the extent that I am currently developing a network called 'Koze Fanm' for women to meet and connect. Through this initiative, I aim to introduce others to the influential women in my life who have inspired me, with the hope of bringing about positive outcomes for more people. This includes leveraging the medium of radio, training, technology, as well as the content of this book, and more.

In addition to my mother, sisters, other relatives, friends, and acquaintances, many women have encouraged me to strive for excellence throughout my career. I am committed to honoring them in everything I do. My ultimate goal is to empower other women to experience the same sense of growth and personal evolution that I have. In the end, it all circles back to the importance of cultivating genuine relationships and connections.

Relationships Can Be Lessons

When I went through a divorce, my ex-husband wasn't as involved with our children as I had hoped he would be. Some people might believe that child support is solely about money, but it goes beyond that. I struggled to convey this concept to him. I desired him to be a more active father, but unfortunately, that wasn't happening. I hoped that as our children grew into young adults, he would naturally become closer to them.

Rather than dwelling on my absent ex-husband and complaining, I decided to take action. I enrolled in NPCL's Building Strong Families program, which is led by Dr. Jeffery M. Johnson in Washington, DC. Through this program, I became a master trainer for fatherhood initiatives and fragile family development. This training equipped me to address my own situation and assist individuals facing similar challenges.

I also applied my training experience by encouraging Haitian fathers to become more involved in their children's lives. I used to organize an annual event through the Alliance for Progress, where we honored fathers of young children in the community. This event served as a way to encourage fathers to stay engaged in their children's lives and set a positive example for other dads. The ultimate goal was to bring families together and provide them with support. I firmly believe that both children and parents benefit from structure and support.

Dealing With Difficult
Situations And People

Sometimes, we must move forward while silently honoring the people in our past, savoring the present moment, and embracing the future with hope. Whether you like it or not, you will encounter difficult people and situations in life. However, dealing with these individuals doesn't have to become a way of life or a burden to carry continuously. Instead, it can be a stepping stone to your success. I've had numerous encounters with difficult people and situations over the years, and I've learned that you truly discover what you're made of and get to know yourself better when you're put to the test.

Navigating encounters with challenging individuals often necessitates care, composure, and maintaining your calm. No matter how difficult someone might be, strive to respect them and refrain from passing judgment.

Here are some reminders for those of us dealing with complicated family relationships:

At times, we wish our family situation were different.

If someone doesn't desire a healthy relationship, it's not solely your responsibility to bring harmony. Instead, focus on healing yourself. Remember, you are not alone, and no family is perfect. It's okay to speak your truth. It's up to you to decide not to engage in unnecessary arguments. Always aim to protect your freedom peace of mind, and improve your overall health and well-being.

Sometimes, when someone behaves difficultly, it's a sign that they have unmet needs, so try not to take it personally. Avoid responding to anger with anger and refrain from talking over the person. As both a mother and a businesswoman, I've learned the importance of allowing the other person to take a breath before I begin speaking. Always remember to maintain your composure. If things escalate, seeking help and considering an exit strategy are perfectly acceptable options.

There have been instances when I've needed to refer difficult people to more qualified professionals to address their business-related struggles.

Establishing boundaries and setting limits are essential for maintaining mutual respect. Make it clear that it's not acceptable for others to speak poorly to you or treat you disrespectfully. Enforce these boundaries by demanding respect and refusing to tolerate condescending or belittling behavior. If you find it challenging to get a word in, inform people that you need a moment to speak because one-sided conversations are not effective.

Dealing with difficult people within your family can be challenging because you can't simply remove them from your life, and the personal nature of these situations can be painful. It takes wisdom to avoid stooping to their level. Don't let them drag you into their storm; instead, strive to maintain your peace. Recognize your self-worth and act accordingly.

It's essential to make an effort not to become a difficult person yourself. Keep yourself in check by practicing mindfulness and, if it aligns with your beliefs, through prayer. If you suspect you might be burdening someone, try to empathize by putting yourself in their shoes and working together to find a solution that benefits both parties. Be vigilant about recognizing when your actions could potentially hurt someone's feelings and make adjustments to avoid causing harm. Maintain control over your emotions to ensure you don't harm those around you.

Sometimes, we endure challenging situations without giving ourselves due credit. The COVID-19 pandemic taught me the value of recognizing and appreciating the adversity I could overcome. Dealing with difficult people often requires a similar level of resilience and self-awareness.

Loving and appreciating ourselves is crucial to keep moving forward. Learn what's best for you and continue on your journey with a smile, whether it's genuine or forced—no one else's opinion matters. Keep creating beautiful memories along the way.

RELATIONSHIPS WITH OUR PEERS

Friendships are complex, but if you intentionally navigate them, they can be beautiful. Be your own best friend first, and remember that the stories you tell yourself and others shape your view of the world. Be careful about what you share and with whom you share your message.

Friends can play an essential role in our lives and well-being. The people we surround ourselves with directly impact how we feel and operate. Given this, you must control who has access to you in any capacity. You have to manage both the energy you allow in and the energy you expend.

Knowing where you stand with your friends is important because not all friendships share the same experience. I've had friends I don't often talk to, but the connection is truly awesome when we do. We pour good things into each other.

However, as I've aged, I've learned not to cut some friends off. This is a lesson that I had to learn, but it took a while for me to understand its value. Keeping yourself busy while working on self-improvement will naturally lead you to distance yourself from those who are not good for you.

Another important thing to recognize is that what you look for in a friend will change as you mature and evolve. What I sought in a friend as a teenager differs from what I seek in a friend in my 40s. When you meet people who could potentially become friends, consider what you can contribute to each other's lives.

In friendship, there is no need to determine who is the leader or follower. The best place for equality is in genuine friendships. Companionship is vital to us, whether it involves having a clever mind to exchange ideas with or sometimes having a shoulder to cry on; it goes a long way.

A true friend shares both joys and sorrows. They are there for every moment. Be mindful that you can find friends within your family; sometimes, your friends can feel like more than family. The bottom line is that there should be mutual respect in every friendship.

Sometimes, we must also learn to avoid drama to find inner peace. In certain situations, we must forgive without explanation and move on. I now know what I want and deserve, so I no longer settle for less.

Throughout my life, I have nurtured numerous successful friendships. To sustain these relationships, it is essential to remain genuine, radiate positivity, and lend an ear when your friend needs it. It's also important to surround yourself with individuals who can sense when something is on your mind, even if you haven't verbalized it. At times, being heard is all we require.

Additionally, it is crucial to prioritize and maintain a positive connection with God.

Reader Reflection

"A friend loves at all times, and a brother is born for a time of adversity." - Proverbs 17:17 (NIV)

Journal Prompts

Healing from past trauma is crucial for your well-being. It empowers you to embrace a more enlightened present, establish deeper connections with others, and radiate an irresistible aura of self-sufficiency. By taking care of yourself in this way, you'll become more desirable and less dependent on others for your happiness. Never give up on yourself.

1. Which relationships do you value the most?

2. How is your communication in relationships? Where could you improve?

3. What are you looking for in a friendship?

Tips to Adjust the Volume

- Question your surroundings.

- Follow your heart.

- Take time to interact with others.

- Take time to create memories.

- Enjoy the present moment.

- Don't let ego kill the vibe.

- In good or challenging moments, find time to sit down to evaluate and talk things through.

CHAPTER SEVEN
Seeing Things in a New Light

Maintaining HOPE during a period of waiting:

Believing in hope is crucial because it instills faith in us that things will eventually get better.

Hope provides us with the ability to recharge,

Hope courage to rebuild,

Hope acts as a calming voice that constantly whispers for us to be still.

Hope also gives us the strength to persevere and rise again.

Make choices for a happier and healthier life, and adopt a more serious approach toward your vision, purpose, and personal growth. Learn from your failures and keep trying. Remember, it takes courage to be unique. Embrace your journey; it belongs uniquely to you, and there's no room for comparison. In due time, you'll realize that wisdom is true wealth and comprehend genuine power. We either win or we learn. I had to reframe my thinking and change my perspective to see things differently in order to continue evolving. We must seize opportunities to level up.

Living with purpose does not guarantee a trouble-free life. Some things that God intends for us to understand only become clear during our darkest times. Be patient while facing life's tests and trials; growth is on the horizon. My faith in God has given me the courage to redirect my energy towards a more positive outcome. I believe that God is my guiding light, and with His guidance, I can achieve great things. Remember that through pain, miracles can be unleashed. For instance, my struggles have led to the transformation of my philosophies into valuable and practical concepts, a shift towards innovation, increased confidence, and a newfound embrace of fresh opportunities. Sometimes, what we perceive as working against us is, in fact, working for our benefit. It's time to cease dwelling on past mistakes. Instead, let's utilize them as opportunities for growth and advancement, enabling us to function at a higher level.

Gaining perspective is a potent tool that can reshape our perception of reality. It's astonishing to see how our mindset shapes the world around us. So, how is your current mindset influencing your reality?

Sometimes, we need to break free from rigid routines that no longer serve us and release commitments that have lost their purpose. It's also crucial to take responsibility for our decisions and evaluate them thoughtfully so that we are taken seriously and can progress. We possess the power to establish healthier patterns, and it's advantageous to begin with small commitments. I've learned that progress takes time, and even under pressure, we can still accomplish our goals.

No matter how much you believe, life has shattered you or wish you had made different choices to evade pain, remember that adversity can break your heart open to refine your vision. When times get tough, recall that past mistakes have shaped the person you are today. The wisdom gained from your experiences is truly invaluable. It is essential not to let others' opinions disrupt your inner peace. Abandon the habit of speaking negatively about yourself and witness the transformative impact it has on your life.

Maintaining a healthy mindset can significantly alter your life's trajectory. It's crucial to understand your emotions and their influence on your well-being. By reflecting on past experiences and looking forward with optimism, you can discover inspiration for the future.

By embracing an attitude of gratitude, we can cultivate greater contentment and a more positive outlook on life. This involves appreciating what we possess, nurturing a positive attitude, living with intention, and trusting that God can accomplish the impossible in His perfect timing. This approach allows us to engage constructively with our past and future. Engaging in mindfulness practices can be particularly beneficial. Since life is a precious gift, we must remain humble and thankful to avoid regrets.

Focusing on the present is an invaluable gift. It's essential to savor each day. Have you heard of mindfulness? Take a moment to reflect on yourself and your aspirations for the future. Mindfulness involves remaining fully present and directing your thoughts toward the current moment. It's crucial to manage our emotions and practice self-discipline for personal growth. This ability allows us to observe what's happening in the present moment without dwelling on the past or worrying about the future. Everyone has unresolved childhood issues that can affect us if left unaddressed. Confronting these issues can help us avoid unintentionally hurting others.

To better understand the significance of mindset and mindfulness, it's important to recognize that our attitude shapes our experiences, which, in turn, shapes our perspective. As Wayne Dyer wisely said, "If you change how you look at things, the things you look at change." Our upbringing and life experiences influence how we naturally perceive our environment. Nothing happens in our lives without some form of invitation.

It's easier to change your mindset than to alter your experiences. Sometimes, choosing silence to maintain peace can be the best approach. Although you can't control your reality, you can manage your attitude toward it. By being mindful of the present, you can act as you choose. Keep in mind that falling into the water won't drown you; it's staying in it that will.

It is our responsibility to control our perspective. Start paying attention to your thoughts and adjust them as needed. By shifting our mindset, we can see things from a different angle or in a different light.

To make progress and adopt a new perspective, we must seek to identify any negative or limiting beliefs that may be holding us back. Once you recognize them, accept them, and take steps toward implementing the necessary changes.

At one point in my life, I struggled with insecurities. However, I came to understand that my insecurities were rooted in fear, an emotion that can lead us to make poor choices. I focused on loving and valuing myself, even celebrating small personal victories to combat this. This shift in mindset changed the way I think and act. It's important to identify the things that bring us joy and make them a regular part of our lives. This helps us find joy even during challenging times. Don't be afraid and stay calm - God will fight for you.

Being in control of our emotions is crucial since they affect our well-being and can impact our health. It's important to train ourselves to manage our emotions effectively, as they may be reflected in our medical records. Once, during a flight from Jacmel to Port-au-Prince, I was placed in the co-pilot seat because that was the only seat available. The flight was supposed to be 15 minutes long, but we were still in the air after 30 minutes, and the other passengers were getting anxious. I overheard the pilot say that he was lost, but I had to keep my composure and assure the passengers that everything was alright. I had to control my emotions and physical reactions to try to keep everyone calm. Eventually, we landed safely after 50 minutes, and it was a relief that no one was unnecessarily stressed. The most important thing was that we landed safely.

As multifaceted individuals fulfilling different roles in society and our personal lives, there inevitably arise moments where we must take a moment to reflect, gather our thoughts, and confidently strive towards positive outcomes for ourselves and those around us. It's not just about titles or positions; what matters is one's character and personality.

As you move forward, it's important to maintain a positive outlook and stay grounded in reality. Remember to give yourself credit for your accomplishments and progress. Shifting your perspective opens up new opportunities for your dreams to become a reality. This shift allows you to break free from stagnation, grow, and view things from a fresh perspective.

We must release limiting beliefs that hold us back, create self-doubt, and make us feel that we are not good enough. We must free ourselves from isolation, find the support and resources to help us grow, and permit ourselves to make effective decisions that will impact our lives.

Life can be full of drama; be careful about what you allow into your mind. Rather than dwelling on rejection or difficulties, it's beneficial to concentrate on the end goal. Your past experiences can serve as a guide to achieving success, and your progress thus far is a testament to your capabilities.

Juggling three shows and working six days a week was a significant challenge. These shows, namely Vwa Diaspora, Koze Fanm, and Youth Talk Show, demanded a great deal of my time, affecting my finances and personal life. Even though my children were involved in the Youth Talk Show on Saturdays, my weekdays were preoccupied with radio work and other contracts.

Due to the high cost of airtime and my responsibilities to support myself and my household, I constantly worked with insufficient rest. Unfortunately, I couldn't dedicate as much time to my children or enjoy frequent vacations."

There was a time when I was unsure about being self-employed. It was becoming increasingly difficult and stressful because I was always working. I had to consider different perspectives and approaches that didn't necessarily align with my original goal, which affected the message of my shows. This, coupled with financial strain, led me to rethink my strategy.

I had to simplify my life by clearing my mind and refocusing to think creatively. This presented a valuable opportunity that significantly impacted my personal and professional life.

During a conversation with a dear friend, he questioned why I was spending so much money buying air time.. I explained that it was similar to investing in real estate or a timeshare, as it provides a platform to share information with the community. It also costs a lot of money to be on the air. Afterward, my son also discussed the importance of finding suitable sponsors to help me succeed in my endeavors. He believes that I am skilled in my field and deserve to achieve greater success.

I started to think about the ROI of the radio career. While I enjoyed being on the radio and sharing resources to empower others, I realized that I also had many other personal and professional obligations to consider. Therefore, I needed to approach the situation with more intelligence and ensure that it made sense for me to continue.

In order to maximize my reach and minimize time and effort, I implemented syndication and scaling-down tactics. I strategically increased my presence across multiple platforms and expanded my brand, Koze Fanm, to include a TV component. This has allowed me to focus more on other business ventures while maintaining a consistent message delivery strategy.

Scaling back appeared to be challenging, but I knew it was necessary. This change allowed me to achieve a more significant impact with fewer resources and less energy, ultimately leading to a more efficient, sustainable approach.

Leaders and doers must prioritize harnessing the power of their mindset and how they choose to use their influence. Our thoughts affect our actions and, in turn, our lives and those around us. To achieve success, it's important to identify triggers and avoid repeating past mistakes. Remember, your thoughts manifest in your reality. Stay aware of your self-talk, and know that even bad experiences can be a part of a greater story. Take the next step towards improvement.

Have you ever observed how mother ducks lead their ducklings? They take off, and their little ones just follow. This behavior is driven by instincts, similar to how humans follow leaders based on their beliefs and values. However, our instincts don't always guarantee that the leader we follow is good or bad.

As an effective leader, it's crucial to establish a constructive atmosphere and guide individuals toward the appropriate path. This entails being adaptable and altering our outlook as needed, depending on the circumstances. Recognizing the proper moments to amplify our message and when to shift our focus can prove instrumental in attaining triumph.

It's beneficial to free ourselves from societal pressures and embrace our true selves as intended by God. We should learn to appreciate what we once wished for and find contentment in what we have. While aspiring to extraordinary goals is admirable, we must also strive for balance and exercise self-control through prayer and personal effort.

Take some time to understand your own emotions, including what brings you happiness, anger, and sadness. Connect with nature, prioritize self-care, and seek inner peace; these steps can help transform your mindset. Remember, a little laughter can go a long way in alleviating our pain.

Laughter has always been my go-to tool for adjusting my mindset, mood, my overall attitude, both on and off the air. Even though I make an effort to keep my personal life separate from my professional life, there was one instance when I let my guard down on air. During a commercial break, my friend Phares Duverne stopped by the station, and his humor was so contagious that I couldn't help but laugh uncontrollably. Despite my best efforts to regain composure, my listeners heard my laughter.

Initially, I thought I had made a grave mistake. While on the air, I typically maintained a serious demeanor and seldom smiled. However, I regularly invited my listeners to share their thoughts on a daily topic or question. One day, callers remarked on how my laughter was contagious and uplifting. Their positive feedback influenced my on-air persona, prompting me to incorporate more joy and positivity into my broadcasts.

Upon receiving a favorable reaction, I realized that conveying my message need not be excessively serious. In fact, the audience's remarks confirmed that they were more receptive to my words. Thus, ladies, it's high time we stopped suppressing our giggles and embraced them.

Sharing your happiness can be powerful. Incorporate gratitude and laughter into your daily routine. Develop different plans to grow and become the person you envision yourself to be in all aspects of life - spiritually, physically, financially, intellectually, and creatively.

As a radio personality, my listeners couldn't see me, so my beauty was not a factor. I discovered that my laughter could play a role in my branding. Using laughter helps me convey my message effectively and connect with my audience. Negativity can hinder love, so focus on spreading positivity and radiating light instead. I've succeeded more by maintaining a positive and happy attitude rather than being serious and stoic. My laughter was able to connect with people on a different level.

Humor plays a significant role in my life and helps me deal with difficult situations. However, it's only sometimes apparent to others that I may be struggling, as their perspective may be limited because we don't always know everything that's going on in someone's life. This can sometimes lead to unrealistic expectations, which can be challenging to manage.

Let's have some fun and smile through tough times. A positive attitude can make all the difference, so keep smiling and believing in yourself. Remember to stay focused on your goals and embrace the challenges that come your way. Life is full of surprises, but we can handle anything that comes our way with grace and positivity. Trust your instincts and know that things will get better with time. We all go through ups and downs, but it's important to keep going and never give up. Remember to always dress up because when you look good, you tend to feel better, show up, and be your best version of yourself. Have faith, be strong enough to let go of what's not working, and keep your eyes on the prize. Patience is key, so remember to be kind to yourself, others, and trust the process.

In retrospect, I've learned that life has a way of working itself out. Every challenge and hardship has a purpose; we must trust in something greater than ourselves. With faith, we can find the reward waiting for us at the end of the road.

Ecclesiastes 7:14

When times are good, be happy; but when times are bad, consider this:

God has made the one as well as the other. Therefore, they are kept from discovering anything about their future.

In January 2020, I embarked on a journey to San Diego, California, to attend life coaching training at the Life Purpose Institute. My goal was to acquire the necessary skills to assist others in uncovering their life purpose. However, during the training, I came to realize that I was the one in need of guidance. This experience emphasized the importance of coaching and helped me appreciate that my struggles had prepared me for my desired future.

Maintaining hope is vital for uplifting your life and living a positive life. It allows you to see the possibilities ahead and empowers you to live better. Although it's not always easy, adjusting your mindset and focusing on the good can help you see things more clearly. Staying positive was challenging at the start of my journey, but I learned to look inward and appreciate my blessings despite setbacks. True joy comes from loving life and finding fulfillment in your actions rather than dwelling on problems. Seek out joy, and it will bring lasting happiness.

I firmly believe in the transformative power of positivity and make it my mission to share hope and optimism for a more fulfilling tomorrow. My passion for spreading positive energy started during my tenure in radio, but it now permeates every aspect of my life as I strive to radiate positivity in all that I do.

Gaining clarity about oneself can aid in discovering humor in life's situations and using them as stepping stones toward progress. Recognizing one's own value is vital for maintaining a positive outlook toward a better future.

Our current experience is likely to have a transformative impact on our personal identities. The circumstances we are currently navigating are prompting shifts within us, and we sincerely hope that these shifts will ultimately lead to positive outcomes.

Set Goals and Be Open to Change

As an individual, I continually strive to enhance myself every day. However, I have come to understand that self-improvement begins with self-acceptance. It is vital to remain true to oneself and avoid pretending to be someone else, as it can have a negative impact on one's mental well-being. To appreciate my current position in my journey, I remain open to new opportunities and strive to do my best in every given situation. I used to struggle with setting boundaries because I would take on too many projects. Now, I recognize that I don't have to handle everything on my own and can rely on others for assistance.

Focus more on the things that bring you a sense of fulfillment and joy. Being aware of when to push forward and when to pull back is crucial for personal growth, development, and peace of mind. In the past, I prioritized making others happy over my own well-being. However, I'm learning that it's acceptable to focus on myself occasionally. Taking care of oneself is essential; it's also good to assist others. However, it's imperative to make self-care a priority in order to serve others better.

Despite the many events of 2020, I remained steadfast in my determination to prioritize what truly matters to me. This unwavering commitment enabled me to establish clear objectives and pursue them through purposeful actions.

I fully understand how setting goals can provide a sense of direction and purpose. It's important to ensure that your goals are achievable, quantifiable, and well-defined so that you can stay on track and work toward fulfilling your aspirations. I know that it can be challenging to balance your current circumstances with your future ambitions, but taking action and putting in the necessary effort is crucial to achieving your desired outcomes. Keep up the great work!

As individuals, we possess a wide range of interests and ambitions that can sometimes take time to prioritize. However, taking that crucial first step towards achieving our goals is vital, as it can open up a world of possibilities. For instance, when I launched my radio show, Koze Fanm, I set a specific debut date. This required careful planning and preparation, including creating a budget, saving funds, and clarifying my objectives. With unwavering determination and hard work, I successfully achieved my desired outcome, which inspired others to pursue their aspirations.

Being a radio host requires the ability to influence people's viewpoints. This demands balance, strength, and focus in order to make a significant impact. I had numerous messages I wanted to convey, making the task of influencing others a crucial aspect of my role. However, finding the right approach and staying true to my calling was challenging. Initially, I struggled with changing others' perspectives.

My journey as a mother has taught me valuable lessons in communication. My children's diverse perspectives challenged me to become a better listener and to appreciate different viewpoints. I have learned to communicate effectively with those who may not see eye to eye with me while still showing them respect and understanding. These lessons have been invaluable in both my personal and professional life.

My objective is to assist individuals in their quest for happiness. From what I have observed, beginning each day with a positive mindset and having faith in a higher power can be crucial in conquering obstacles. It's important to acknowledge the wisdom of a higher power and to keep in mind that you have support.

It is recommended to regularly take a moment to reflect and be thankful, even for difficult situations, as they can lead to positive outcomes through God's help. Consider your personal goals and how you can positively impact the present using your unique talents and abilities.

Recognizing your self-worth and making necessary adjustments to achieve your goals and responsibilities is essential. Discipline can bring positive outcomes into your life. Remember that your current thoughts shape your future, so seek happiness and inner peace. Adversities teach valuable lessons that can help you grow. Embrace peace, love, and joy.

Keep in mind that being too busy and stressed can harm your health, so prioritize self-care.

Cultivating your personal skills can help you navigate difficult situations and foster healthier coping mechanisms. Through my faith, I've gained clarity and can see the divine plan for my life. God is always present to provide and protect us, even in challenging times. Letting go of outdated beliefs and regulations can help us reach our full potential. Practicing self-love and acceptance can lead to greater confidence. Trusting in God's plan can help release power from things that once bothered us.

Have faith, be confident, own your decisions and choices. These are keys to gaining power, achieving success, and becoming independent. Dwelling on past mistakes will only lead to regret. Believe in the positive affirmations of what God has for you and embrace your true self to live a fulfilling life. Remember that you are destined for greatness. Even if you don't feel it now, take action, prepare yourself, and seize the day. You have the potential to accomplish amazing things.

Understandably, your past decisions have influenced your current situation. Recognizing where you are now and taking steps toward a positive future is important. As you make choices, ask yourself if they align with your desired life. Remember, determination and perseverance can lead to great rewards, just as seen in stories from the Bible and real-life experiences. You've got this.

I aim to embrace life fully while valuing every stage of my journey as I transition into a new phase of my life. Moreover, I plan to utilize my experiences, lessons, and wisdom to assist people in confronting their apprehension of growing old with more courage and self-assurance.

As you gain more experience, your perspective tends to change. While many of us would like to hold on to our youth, it's not how life works. It's okay to embrace the feeling of being young as long as we accept our maturity.

Each season in our life comes with different circumstances, and we must adjust our style based on our current seasons. We must embrace the challenges that come with each season and adjust accordingly.

In retrospect, we can identify alternative approaches that could have been taken to address the challenges we encountered if we had possessed the knowledge we do now. As we evolved and developed, we began to appreciate the difficulties we confronted. However, there are certain things that we must not tolerate, such as agreeing to conditions that do not serve our best interests, neglecting our own needs, and making excuses for the unacceptable actions of others.

Both learning and teaching are essential for my personal growth and development. Education is not limited to attending college; it involves having an open mindset and enhancing our emotional intelligence. Nowadays, there are numerous ways to gain knowledge and skills. Though earning a degree is beneficial, investing in personal growth and continuous learning is equally valuable. Knowledge is very powerful because once acquired, it cannot be taken away from us.

As we continue to grow and evolve, it's important to recognize that each of us possesses unique leadership qualities. The key is discovering our strengths and finding the best ways to utilize them. Remember that just because someone else excels in a particular area, it doesn't mean we will, too. We all have our own individual paths, purposes, and destinies to fulfill in this life.

As the youngest in my family, I often felt like I couldn't measure up to my older sisters because they were already grown. Along the way, I learned that comparing myself to others only brings me down. Instead, I forged my own path and created my unique identity. It's important to remember that we all have our own strengths and weaknesses, which make us who we are. Embrace your individuality and live your life to the fullest. You are capable of achieving great things.

Certain straightforward actions can significantly impact your mindset. Here are some suggestions that you can begin implementing immediately:

- Embrace your individuality.
- Make time for yourself.
- Know that you're enough.
- Make every day count because we never know when it will be the last one.
- You've come a long way, so don't take your experience and pain for granted.
- Find ways to help others.
- Chew your food slowly and practice mindful eating.
- Enjoy the things that you once prayed for.
- Learn to accept rejections but never give up.
- Acknowledge disappointment and pain, but don't allow them to control your emotions.

Adapting to new practices during these challenging times can understandably be difficult. However, it's crucial that we shift our mindset and recognize our ability to overcome these obstacles. Let's focus on the positive aspects and strive toward our goals, finding joy in every step of the journey.

The COVID-19 pandemic undeniably emphasized the importance of adopting a fresh perspective when facing adversity. While this global health crisis has undoubtedly affected individuals in various ways, it's imperative to maintain a positive outlook and remain hopeful for a return to normalcy. I took this opportunity to invest in myself by enrolling in various courses and training programs to improve my skills.

Despite the challenges the pandemic has brought, I feel blessed to have grown closer to God during this time. This has given me the courage to share my light with my loved ones and my audience. We have also learned that we are stronger than we thought. While some aspects of my businesses were negatively impacted, I am grateful for remaining healthy.

To tackle the challenges of our time, we must have faith in asking the Holy Spirit to guide us and be open to new perspectives, diverse ideas, and innovative approaches. By being courageous and self-assured, we have the power to fearlessly overcome any obstacle that confronts us. Hebrews 13:6 (NIV) says, 'So that we may boldly say, The Lord is my helper, and I will not fear what man shall do unto me.'

Despite the occasional obstacles I faced, I remained determined to infuse positivity into my show. It was of utmost importance for me to maintain a hopeful outlook to inspire those in my vicinity. This required me to adapt and maintain a positive attitude.

I completely understand the significance of uplifting messages and have personally experienced the positive impact they can have. While staying informed about current events, I have found it helpful to remain impartial and view situations objectively. It's all about maintaining a balanced perspective.

During these challenging times, we must prioritize our well-being. I've found mindfulness to be incredibly beneficial. It's amazing to see how a clear mind enables you to approach things more positively and adaptable. On a related note, how do you feel about prayer in your life? Does it hold significant meaning for you?

Reading Reflection

"A cheerful heart is good medicine, but a crushed spirit dries up the bones." - Proverbs 17:22 (NIV)

"The Lord is my light and my salvation— whom shall I fear? The Lord is the stronghold of my life— of whom shall I be afraid?" - Psalm 27 (NIV)

"When I was a child, I talked like a child, I thought like a child, I reasoned like a child. When I became a woman, I put the ways of childhood behind me." - 1 Corinthians 13 (NIV)

"For I know the plans I have for you," declares the Lord, "plans to prosper you and not to harm you, plans to give you hope and a future." - Jeremiah 29:11 (NIV)

"Emancipate yourselves from mental slavery None but ourselves can free our minds Have no fear for atomic energy cause none of them can stop time." - Bob Marley

"The LORD is my shepherd, I lack nothing. He makes me lie down in green pastures, He leads me beside quiet waters, he refreshes my soul. He guides me along the right paths for his name's sake. Even though I walk through the darkest valley, I will fear no evil, for you are with me; your rod and your staff, they comfort me. You prepare a table before me in the presence of my enemies. You anoint my head with oil; my cup overflows. Surely your goodness and love will follow me all the days of my life, and I will dwell in the house of the LORD forever." - Psalms 23:1-6 (NIV)

Journal Prompts

1. How have you had to shift your perspective for your own happiness or peace of mind?

2. How is your perspective affecting your current reality?

3. What people, situations or events caused you to feel sad or angry?

Tips to Adjust the Volume

- Use energy to believe in the infinite possibilities mindset.

- Focus on your strength.

- Keep learning about yourself to build a stronger character.

- No matter what, find something to be grateful for.

- When you are true to yourself, you become more responsible.

CHAPTER EIGHT
Motherhood: The Never-Ending Lesson

I grew up believing that children would give meaning to my life. I also realized that being a mother is a significant responsibility and a blessing. There's this bond where we carry our children for nine months, eager to see what we will deliver. And when the time finally arrives, and we are in labor, we are told to push through the pain. It's such a beautiful lesson about being hopeful and finding joy when we face challenges in life.

The journey of raising children is worth remembering and cherishing. When my children were little, we did not have camera phones or social media. However, some of the funny things they used to do are still being mentioned and remembered. As a parent, I have accumulated a wealth of knowledge through the experience of raising my children."

Have you ever considered who has the most significant impact on your life? In life, things will change, and our children will grow and evolve. Take time to enjoy the present moment. It is widely acknowledged that poor parenting and neglect can adversely affect children. However, being a good parent requires hard work, courage, focus, and care. Being a mother has been an incredibly fulfilling and enriching experience for me. Carrying and giving birth to my children was a blessing that taught me much about myself and my capacity to love and grow. While I am not an expert on motherhood, it has made me more mindful of my actions. I have nurtured my children since they were in my womb and have watched them blossom into remarkable individuals. Despite the pain and difficulties of childbirth, it demonstrated to me how perseverance can lead to something beautiful. Motherhood profoundly transforms every aspect of life. Creating life and watching my children grow is a privilege and a miracle I will always treasure.

Becoming a mother and having two children within a short period presented its share of challenges. However, I am grateful for the journey and the strength it has given me. When I see myself in the mirror, I am constantly reminded of my resilience and ability to overcome obstacles and how God's favor is upon me. My children, Jonathan and Natalie, are the love of my life, and I cherish every moment of our shared adventure, even with its imperfections. Being a mother is an honor I hold in high regard, and I approach it confidently and gratified.

Reflecting on the past as a parent with grown children, it's clear that while we can offer guidance, it's ultimately up to our children to make their own decisions and choices with their free will. Ensuring the safety and well-being of your loved ones while savoring precious moments with your young ones is of utmost importance. Appreciate what you have without waiting for perfection.

Being a responsible parent necessitates a robust support system, whether it's a single parent or both parents working together. A community of individuals, including the mother, father, siblings, grandparents, aunts, uncles, and others, is indispensable in laying a solid foundation for our children. Let us work collaboratively to provide our children with the best possible support.

As we evolve into our desired selves, we can impart our acquired skills to our children, helping them avoid repeating our past mistakes. We can share valuable insights from our missteps and those of others, sparing them unnecessary pain, as my mom used to tell me, though I understand it better now. However, they may not be able to grasp the message right away. This involves establishing clear boundaries and providing our children with appropriate guidance on how to conduct themselves.

Just remember that we have to lead by example. Colin Powell, the former U.S. Secretary of State, once said, "We can seldom get our children to do what we tell them, but they seldom fail to imitate us." Show your love, teach them resilience, and instill self-respect.

As responsible parents, we must recognize the significance of setting boundaries for our children. While the younger generation may appear more sensitive and emotional than our own, we must consciously try to comprehend their struggles. Establishing personal connections with them can provide valuable insight into their experiences. Responding intentionally to their problems and demonstrating a genuine interest in their outlook on the world is crucial. By doing so, we can make a positive impact on their lives. Give it a try and witness the transformation for yourself.

As responsible adults, we understand the challenges we face in these unprecedented times. The current situation can be overwhelming with the ongoing pandemic, social distancing, and the Black Lives Matter movement. It is important that we approach these obstacles collaboratively and constructively. Doing so can set a positive example for our children and help them emerge from these challenges stronger than ever.

As a fellow single parent, I understand the importance of making thoughtful and responsible decisions that benefit you and your children in the long run. It's crucial to show your kids love and respect while encouraging their individuality, as this can help build a healthy relationship. When I went through a similar situation and realized my marriage wasn't working, I knew it wouldn't be easy to become a single parent. However, through prayers, discipline, and support from family and friends, I was able to make the transition smoother for my children.

Becoming a mother had always been my dream while growing up, and it finally came true. My first child was a boy, and my second was a girl. The journey was not without its difficulties. I got married at 21 in Haiti and later moved back to the United States, where I gave birth to my son when I was 23 and my daughter when I was 24. It was challenging to have two babies within a year.

During that season of my life, I experienced a range of emotions. The arrival of my children coincided with my youth and separation from my family. As I began to discover my identity, the presence of these two little souls in my life transformed everything.

I felt a lot of stress when I was alone with two babies in a foreign country. My ex-husband lost his job just days after our son was born. I lived in New Jersey while some of my loved ones were in New York and Haiti.

Back then, making long-distance calls was expensive, and due to our financial difficulties, it was challenging to stay in touch with anyone besides my ex-husband and some relatives from his side of the family. As a result, I felt isolated and lacked adequate support.

A Mother's Internal Struggles

No one can hide pain better than a mother. We always strive to hold ourselves together to ensure the comfort of others. After the birth of my first son, I managed to persevere despite the challenges when my daughter arrived just ten months later. This period was exceptionally demanding for us, compounded by my ex-husband's unemployment, which had lasted for a few months by then. I became overwhelmed with anxiety, leading to erratic eating and disrupted sleep patterns. Amidst all this stress, I found myself unable to breastfeed my daughter.

The overwhelming stress and profound sense of loneliness I experienced were something I couldn't comprehend at the time. It wasn't until later that I realized I had undiagnosed postpartum depression (PPD), a form of perinatal depression.

Perinatal depression encompasses depression that begins during pregnancy, known as prenatal depression, and depression that arises after the baby is born, referred to as postpartum depression. Mothers grappling with perinatal depression often face extreme sadness, anxiety, and fatigue that can impede their ability to carry out daily tasks, including self-care and caring for others.

According to a study conducted by the Postpartum Depression organization, approximately 1 out of 7 women experience PPD within a year of giving birth. It's important to note that PPD is not synonymous with the commonly experienced "baby blues," which typically occur within the first two weeks of a child's life.

I realized I likely had PPD when I shared my experience many years later while working on the radio. I was involved in various segments on a show sponsored by the Children Services Council of Broward County, and during one episode, a guest discussed PPD. It was during this conversation that I opened up about my own experience to my dear friend Andrew Leone, the former Director of Communication and Community Outreach at CSC. He was the first person to ever mention PPD to me.

Once I came to the realization that I had likely experienced this condition without a formal diagnosis, I dedicated a segment of my show to sharing resources for other mothers, ensuring they could access the help they needed. The Children's Services Council of Broward County has a program to assist mothers experiencing PPD, so I invited specialists from this organization to join my show.

PPD is not something any woman should have to face alone. I understand that, in general, Black, Hispanic, and Caribbean women often feel compelled to hide their mental health issues due to cultural stigmas. However, it's important to recognize that we owe it to ourselves to seek help during challenging times. I strongly encourage other women experiencing PPD to reach out to their medical professionals and loved ones for support. Discover what brings you comfort and make self-care a top priority.

I overcame undiagnosed PPD by making a significant change in my life. When my daughter was two months old, and my son was around a year old, I packed up my two infants and traveled to Haiti. This temporary move became a crucial step in my healing process. Surrounded by family, I went from feeling unsupported to being uplifted.

Looking back at that time, I see it as a profound transition from being a young adult to becoming a mother and evolving as a person. I gained invaluable insights about myself during that challenging chapter in my life. Although it was tough at the time, that experience played a pivotal role in shaping the woman I am today. We all face traumas in our lives, but the best gift you can give yourself and your children is the gift of healing.

While it might seem easier said than done, don't shy away from difficult circumstances because they are the crucibles that reveal your true self. As unfortunate as these situations may be, they have the potential to help you understand who you are and what you are truly capable of.

Things I Wish I Knew

There are many things I wish I had known before becoming a mother, especially regarding the importance of maintaining my health through nutrition and healthy habits. While I was excited about motherhood, I lacked precise knowledge on how to prepare myself for this life-altering role. I would have preferred to learn how to be physically, intellectually, and emotionally ready for the profound experience of motherhood.

Becoming a mother is an ongoing journey, and there's no going back to how things were before. Life unfolds rapidly, and you encounter numerous surprises along the way. Often, we find ourselves trying to meet everyone's needs and understand them, neglecting our own well-being. However, by taking care of ourselves and setting healthy boundaries, we can better serve others.

I quickly realized that raising a boy and a girl, each with unique personality required significant support. I turned to God for guidance and leaned on my "village." Alongside my family, my church community played a crucial role in my journey. My sisters, especially in the early stages, were phenomenal. Over two decades later, I'm still learning how to parent these two distinct individuals, but the lessons I've gathered along the way have been invaluable.

There were some challenges along the road. When my kids were 9 and 10, I went through a divorce. As mothers, we often tend to be more caring, even though kids may be more obedient to their fathers. Recognizing that my marriage was failing, I knew I had to change my approach and establish boundaries so that my kids would listen to me more when I needed to discipline them. I made this shift early on, realizing that it would help ease the transition when I eventually had to leave my husband.

Mothers are nurturers, and fathers are disciplinarians. I had to become both. As a Black mother, I always feared that my daughter would get pregnant early or my son would end up in jail or not finish high school. I desperately wanted to shield my children from falling into stereotypes or becoming statistics. Although both of my children turned out well, there were moments along the way that validated some of my fears.

As parents, we often tend to be overprotective of our children. When my kids were teenagers, a friend told me, "Black women raise girls and love boys." This idea stuck with me. I made an effort not to stifle their growth as they grew older by being overly protective. I realized the importance of allowing our children to grow and have their own experiences while supporting them and reminding them that they are capable, loved, and believed in.

I have shared some of my stories and life experiences with my children, but I've delved deeper into these discussions with my daughter, Natalie, as she transitioned into young adulthood. I aim not to dictate what she should or shouldn't do. I hope that she can make sound judgments about the people she chooses to be with, learning from her own experiences and those of others. Nonetheless, I consistently emphasize the importance of self-worth to her.

Despite our differences, I make an effort not to demonize or blame their father. I've been honest with them about our relationship and encouraged them to maintain a healthy relationship with him in their own way.

I wish my ex-husband had been more present when the children were younger, but I strive not to hold onto grudges. I often remind my children that holding grudges is like drinking poison and hoping the other person will suffer. Forgiveness is a practice I try to live by for our own well-being and relief.

Fostering the relationship between my kids and their dad not only benefited them but also helped me address my childhood issues with my own father despite his passing many years ago. My father was only present in my life from the age of five until I turned twelve. I'm grateful for the values he instilled in me during that time. While I'm unsure why he chose that specific period to be a part of my life, I now recognize that those years played a significant role in shaping the person I am today. It was all worth it.

Forgiveness is just one of the principles I aimed to instill in my children. I always emphasize to them that the challenges they face won't last forever. I also make it a point to remind them regularly that they hold great importance in my life and that I love them dearly. Since they were young, I've made it clear that family and education are of utmost importance.

When my children were younger, our relationships were harmonious. However, as they entered their teenage years, our connections became strained at times. This experience taught me the importance of controlling my emotions while navigating various situations with my children. I've learned to address emotional wounds in a way that doesn't negatively impact my relationships with them or hinder our future together. I've embraced the lessons and let go of emotions that no longer serve a purpose.

The constantly evolving dynamic between my children and me underscores the unique nature of motherhood. Over the past two decades, I've taken on the roles of both teacher and student. My daughter taught me patience, especially during the challenging moments in her younger years. My son heightened my awareness; he used to ensure I was fully engaged during our conversations by seeking my attention and making sure I was listening.

Motherhood has changed me in countless ways. It taught me the importance of cherishing each moment because children grow up so quickly. When my kids were younger, my mother always emphasized the significance of spending more time with them. Unfortunately, I didn't take her advice seriously soon enough. I was constantly working, ensuring that we had food on the table and a safe place to live. I distinctly remember when my son was just two months old, and I wish I had savored that time more. I also recall when Natalie was a year and a half old, she began to talk and exhibit curiosity. I wish I had been more attentive to them. Nowadays, people have the advantage of having cameras on their phones and social media to share their stories. All I have are my memories, which I cherish dearly. These memories are truly priceless. My advice to you is simple: "Make every moment count."

Throughout this journey, our perception of ourselves undergoes significant changes. It's up to you to shape the image that makes you more self-aware and enlightened. Embracing change more openly will enable you to lead a happier life. By shifting our awareness, we become more comfortable with the realization that everything changes.

Motherhood has taught me a great deal about love, encouraging me to be more thoughtful, hopeful, and motivated. It has provided me with a unique perspective on life and made me realize that I am content with the choices I've made. Even though I believe I did a good job as a mother to both of my children, I must admit that mother's guilt is a real thing. There are times when I think I could've done better. However, I also recognize that I can't go back and change certain things, so I try not to dwell on them. Beating myself up would not improve the situation, especially when it concerns events from the past. I also want to give myself credit because when I talked to my children about their childhood experiences and what they shared, it wasn't as bad as I had feared.

Motherhood has profoundly influenced my identity and forged a strong bond between my mother and me. There's a Haitian saying that goes, "animals with tails don't fly over fires," which implies that there are certain things one should avoid when raising children. Since becoming a mother, I've had to think twice before I act or react to certain situations. At times, it feels like I'm living in a glass house, and I've developed a heightened sense of responsibility because I know my children are always watching.

I grew up observing my mom working diligently, and staying at home was not part of her cultural norm. As a working mom, I often found myself exhausted and overwhelmed. There were numerous programs and extracurricular activities I wished I could have enrolled my children in, but time constraints made it challenging. Being a single mother added an extra layer of difficulty since I didn't have a partner to share the load.

When my kids were younger, they always wanted to share their experiences with me or play when I returned home from work. However, after preparing dinner and checking their homework, I often retreated to my room because it was quite overwhelming after a long day. Despite my deep love for my children, I frequently thought, "I wasn't prepared for this, but I've managed." Nevertheless, the challenges I've faced have molded me into the person I am today.

Understandably, mothers may feel guilty, but it's crucial to prioritize enjoying each moment and not letting those feelings consume you. Remember, it's okay to take care of yourself as well.

As a mother, I constantly reinvent myself and improve my negotiation skills. The 2008-2009 market crash presented challenges as my home was going into foreclosure, and I had to file for bankruptcy. To avoid any disruption in my children's lives and having to move somewhere else, I decided to short-sell the house to a buyer who agreed to let me rent it back from her. Finding a new place to live was difficult due to credit issues, but I was committed to providing my children with a safe and stable environment until they became young adults.

It's important to remember that the challenges we encounter today can help us grow stronger in the future. I've found a greater appreciation for life and a more profound capacity for love. Watching my children grow up reminds me of the beauty and goodness in the world and how much guidance I've received from a higher power. My prior work as an interpreter at the Broward County Courthouse has made me more mindful as a parent, realizing the struggles of other families.

One day, I came home from work and learned that the kids' caretaker had instructed them to do something they knew might displease me. My son respectfully refused to comply, stating that his mom was the leader of the house. That made me feel good because it showed me that children pay more attention to the directions given to them than you might think; sometimes, they just need to know why.

Looking back, I now cherish every moment of raising my children. I must admit I didn't always feel this way when they were teenagers.

Mothers, keep believing, keep praying, and have faith. Motherhood is a beautiful journey that never ends. Although my kids are grown, I never stop thinking, worrying, or praying for them. I was afraid to become a mother, but my biggest fear became my greatest blessing. The fear never goes away, but it does change over time. Through prayer, you can become a better parent, manage yourself, and always maintain hope.

Never stop sharing your faith, experiences, or knowledge with your children. One day, my son Jonathan gave me a New Testament Bible. He told me they had given it to him at the Army recruiting office. That gift made my day, and I told him that the first time I received a similar Bible was when I was twelve years old, during my visit to Assemble Shalom Baptiste Fundamental in Haiti as a first-time guest.

The note that he wrote was such a thoughtful and priceless gift that Jonathan could have given me. I also shared with him this Bible passage:

Psalm 23:1-6 (NIV)

Psalms of David,

"The Lord is my shepherd, I lack nothing. He makes me lie down in green pastures, he leads me beside quiet waters, He refreshes my soul. He guides me along the right paths for his name's sake. Even though I walk through the darkest valley, I will fear no evil, for you are with me; your rod and your staff, they comfort me. You prepare a table before me in the presence of my enemies. You anoint my head with oil; my cup overflows. Surely your goodness and love will follow me all the days of my life, and I will dwell in the house of the Lord Forever."

My mom encouraged me to learn this verse by heart and pass it on to my children. As a mother, nothing can trouble you more than your racing thoughts about how well your children are doing. She knew that nobody hides pain better than mothers and that it's important to lean on God's words.

We also need to be aware that our kids will grow and mature into responsible adults as we ourselves are getting older. What we can do for the best is to release them to experience whatever is meaningful to them and free ourselves to take time to enjoy life and the things that are meaningful to us. So, let's practice love, understanding, and positive intentions.

There's no greater reward than being a mother. Don't wait for everything to be perfect before you decide to enjoy the life God has given you. Start experiencing joy, favor, and blessings from God.

Reader Reflection

To all mothers reading this, try not to let negative thoughts consume your mind. If you're facing challenges with your children right now, ask God to give you patience and wisdom, always pray for them. Young people today are dealing with many adversities, disappointments and temptations, desperate for validation. They are trying to figure out their own life. Even as parents, we don't always have it figured out, and we are not perfect.

Isaiah 40:31 NIV

But those who hope in the LORD will renew their strength. They will soar on wings like eagles; they will run and not grow weary, they will walk and not be faint.

Journal Prompts

1. How has parenthood shaped your life?

2. What lessons have you learned from your children?

3. How have you transformed yourself to better provide for your children?

4. Are you taking steps to heal yourself from past trauma?

5. Are you open to coaching, training and therapy?

Tips to Adjust the Volume

- Start taking yourself more seriously.
- Set firm boundaries.
- Verbalize your boundaries.
- Allow your kids to grow and treat them accordingly.
- Don't save your compliments for later. Let them know that you are proud of them.

CHAPTER NINE
Negotiation for Clarification

L ife is a series of choices, negotiations, and strategic moves. It's essential to learn and practice the art of having supportive conversations. Ask God to grant you the gift of discernment, as He possesses all-encompassing knowledge.

It's valuable to clearly define the issues at hand during negotiations and identify your positions in life when you aim to maximize the benefits for yourself and others. Take a moment to reflect on what holds significance for you. Conduct a personal assessment to gain a deeper understanding of your needs and values. Be mindful of your intentions, seek compromises, and practice self-awareness while adjusting your strategies accordingly.

Effective negotiation entails engaging in constructive dialogues with individuals or groups to identify mutually beneficial solutions and reach a consensus. I always strive for outcomes that benefit all parties involved, prioritizing collective success over personal gain at the expense of others. Helping others succeed ultimately benefits me as well.

As a woman of Haitian and Caribbean descent, I consider myself fortunate to have been exposed to the art of negotiation from a young age. I had the privilege of observing my mother skillfully bargaining with market vendors, which instilled in me the significance of this skill. Negotiation holds a pivotal role in achieving favorable outcomes across various aspects of life, whether it be in business, romantic partnerships, parenting, or personal relationships. The approach one takes toward a specific situation can indeed determine the success of the negotiations.

Over the years, I have learned some helpful negotiation practices that I want to share.

1. Put your feelings aside and acknowledge the facts.

2. Don't show your desperation.

3. Don't be desperate to get what you're demanding.

4. Don't be afraid of the answer "no."

5. It is good to learn how to negotiate because some wars could have been avoided if people knew how to sit down and discuss their problems.

6. Weigh the options between war and peace, good and bad, highs and lows.

7. Always ask how you can incorporate "win-win" to a better outcome.

It is crucial to keep in mind that you have the ability to take charge of your life. You hold the power to welcome individuals in, make adjustments as needed, and prioritize your thoughts and focus based on your personal preferences.

Negotiation as a Parent

When it comes to negotiating with your children, it's essential to approach them with love and support. As a parent, I've gained valuable insights from my children, Jonathan and Natalie. Parenting requires effective leadership, and it's vital to demonstrate self-leadership to our children because they closely observe our behaviors. Setting a positive example is crucial.

As you guide your children's education, it's important to let them know that you always have their best interests in mind. Teach them about responsibility and the potential outcomes of their decisions. Raising children according to a set of rules can be challenging and requires constant communication, affection, and empathy.

As an advocate for positive parenting, it's important for parents to negotiate with their children and allow them to make choices. However, it's equally important to establish boundaries as adults and help children understand that their actions can have consequences. Sometimes, it could be as simple as setting expectations for their behavior.

Teaching children how to use money as a negotiation tool can be beneficial, but it must be done responsibly. When my kids turned twelve, I gave them the opportunity to purchase their school uniforms and provided each of them with $500 to cover necessary supplies, uniforms, shoes, and other essentials for the academic year. It was fascinating to observe how resourcefully they managed their funds.

From personal experience, I've come to appreciate the importance of responsible spending, particularly when it comes to back-to-school supplies. This valuable lesson has also benefited my children, as they've developed a better understanding of financial management and ownership. Allowing them to make their own purchasing decisions and utilize their own funds has instilled in them a deeper appreciation for the things they own.

Negotiation in Business

In the business world, women may encounter challenges in obtaining the recognition and compensation they rightfully deserve. Therefore, it is crucial to refine one's negotiation skills. Whether working towards a sale, partnership, or collaboration, the ability to negotiate effectively is indispensable. It enables the successful development and maintenance of business relationships, whether you are buying or selling.

The impact of the pandemic affected my business, as it did for many others. During this time, we had to engage in negotiations to pave the way for a brighter future.

It's important to be honest and upfront if you are unable to make payments for a product or service. Communicate with the other party and let them know when they can expect your payments or any other agreed-upon exchange. This transparent approach helps build trust and fosters the possibility of continued business cooperation in the future. Always remember communication is key.

Tips for Negotiating in Business

1. Be fair in negotiation.
2. Trust in yourself.
3. Be respectful and demand respect.
4. Validate the other party and make them feel important.
5. Be truthful in the deal you're working on.
6. Present yourself as your best self.
7. Only make a deal when you know you can comply with the terms.
8. Express yourself with confidence and compassion.
9. Care enough to listen. Remember that you have two ears and one mouth. Listen twice as much as you speak.
10. Be mindful of the other parties involved when negotiating your terms.
11. Keep your eye on the prize. What is it that you want to achieve in your negotiations?
12. Work to transform the issue you're negotiating to get what you need.
13. Ask yourself if what you're negotiating for will work towards improving the situation. Will it elevate the lives of both you and others?
14. Pay close attention to the other person's words, actions, and demeanor.
15. Use visual aids and memory aids as powerful negotiating tools.

Negotiation in Relationships

Romantic relationships typically rely on mutual respect, understanding, and shared benefits. Although there can be cases of unhealthy or abusive dynamics, these should be avoided. It's crucial to prioritize mutual respect and understanding in any healthy relationship.

Navigating relationships can be challenging, so it's essential to take some time to reflect on your goals and priorities before diving in. Understanding what you want from life can help you communicate more clearly with your partner and work together to build a healthy relationship. Remember that compromise is vital in any partnership, and taking the time to establish a solid foundation can make all the difference in the long run.

Effective communication is crucial in all areas of life. To become a better listener, speak less and listen more. Take time to process information before reacting impulsively. It's also important to be aware of others' past experiences as they can impact their reactions and emotions in the present.

It's important to understand how they process emotions and try to empathize with their partner's perspective. Avoid making assumptions and be patient. Establish clear boundaries and pay close attention to their verbal and nonverbal cues to better understand their needs.

To maintain a healthy relationship, it's crucial to balance meeting the other person's desires with your own needs. Start by understanding your own values and limitations. Be practical and honest about what you can provide and what you expect in return. It's essential to ensure that your partner can also fulfill your needs in the relationship. Therefore, clarifying your goals before entering into a partnership is crucial.

It's important to consider whether you and your partner are working towards the same goal. This will determine the strength of your relationship.

For many individuals who support their families, their homes serve as a place of refuge and tranquility. These individuals work tirelessly to provide for their loved ones and seek a peaceful environment to return to. In households where both partners contribute financially, it is important to recognize and adapt to this cultural shift to maintain a harmonious dynamic.

Non–Negotiable in Life

It's vital to find your own path to happiness and never settle for anything less than the best version of yourself. This season offers the perfect opportunity to focus on personal growth and positive energy. Take some time to prioritize self-care and inspire others to do the same. Let's all strive to reach our full potential together!

Life is filled with unspoken understandings; however, we must communicate our expectations clearly. Our behavior plays a crucial role, and we must learn to exercise self-control, which is essential for personal empowerment. While life involves numerous negotiations, it's perfectly acceptable to have certain non-negotiables. I want to emphasize the significance of integrity once again; it holds the utmost importance for me, and I will never compromise it for any reason.

During my marriage, I faced several challenges. My ex-husband was unemployed and studying full-time, while I was only working part-time. On top of that, the car we shared posed transportation challenges. One day, someone I knew offered me $20,000 to buy a new car. Although it would have been helpful, I felt hesitant to accept it because it could have made me vulnerable to blackmail or damaged my reputation. One question that my parents taught me is, 'What are the consequences or the price to pay?' Ultimately, I decided not to take the money because I didn't want to compromise my integrity or jeopardize future relationships. It's crucial to consider the consequences of our choices, as they can shape our lives. We can find solace in our Heavenly Father, who has an infinite supply to help us overcome any difficulty.

Absolutely, it's important to approach situations with a positive outlook and carefully consider the consequences of our actions before making any decisions. This thoughtful approach enables us to make wise choices that ultimately lead to positive outcomes.

Reader Reflection

"They will be like a tree planted by the water that sends out its roots by the stream. It does not fear when heat comes; its leaves are always green. It has no worries in a year of drought and never fails to bear fruit." - Jeremiah 17:8 (NIV)

Journal Prompts

It's important to know what you're trying to accomplish when negotiating.

1. Is negotiating with yourself a good idea? Why or why not?

2. What are your non-negotiables?

Tips to Adjust the Volume

- Know what you are negotiating for.
- Don't be afraid to ask for what you want.
- Don't be in a hurry, be patient, and remember that it's a process.
- Stay focused on what the outcome will be.
- Shut up and listen.
- Position yourself to grow.
- Show the other person that you care about their needs.
- Don't let your ego get in the way of your success.

CHAPTER TEN
Create the Life You Want

Proverbs, chapter 23, verse 7:
"As a man think in his heart, so is he."

W e must understand that we all can learn something from each oth-er. Approaching life with a positive mindset is very helpful in achieving greatness. Some of the questions we encounter in life may take time to yield logical answers. Be patient and utilize your critical thinking skills to shape the life you desire. However, it's essential to find contentment in what you currently possess while working with your existing re-sources. Live in the present moment and savor the peaceful moments.

When aspiring to design the life you desire, it's crucial to learn from past failures and maintain an attitude of gratitude. Additionally, posi-tioning yourself for growth, enjoying the journey, and nurturing pos-itivity are equally important. Sometimes, life requires us to reposition ourselves to discover the necessary light.

As an example, my daughter gifted me a small tomato plant for my birthday. After a few days, the leaves began to wither due to a lack of exposure to sunlight. By changing its position within a few days, I wit-nessed a transformation and observed new growth.

Gratitude can have a profound impact on our lives, and it's worthwhile to actively seek reasons for gratitude every day. Avoid succumbing to the pressure of trying to impress others, such as spending money you don't have or making poor choices, as these actions can lead to unnec-essary stress, anxiety, and depression, negatively affecting our overall well-being. Redirect your energy towards activities and pursuits that bring you genuine joy.

Always remember that your health is your true wealth, and aligning your actions with your plans is crucial for leading a joyful life. Take moments to reflect on your progress and the hurdles you've overcome, and trust that everything will ultimately work out in your favor. Eliminating what doesn't work is the simplest path to creating the life you desire.

Make a firm commitment to embracing virtuous values, appreciating what you already have while striving for more, and focusing on the person you aspire to become. Aim to infuse your consciousness and daily affairs with freedom and joy.

Now is the time to build your authentic self and discover the person you truly want to be. Keep in mind that a clear mind leads to better decision-making and a greater sense of inner peace. Consider your top priorities in life and identify the small steps you can take today to start improving your life.

What are your most significant priorities in life, and what simple actions can you initiate right this moment to enhance your well-being and happiness?

Recently, I learned a valuable lesson from a child. Whenever he dislikes something on TV, he asks his parents to change it immediately. This made me realize that I, too, can change my energy channel and shift my attitude whenever necessary.

We should continually draw lessons from our past experiences, knowledge, and wisdom to become smarter individuals. Sometimes, we must carefully weigh the short-term and long-term consequences when making decisions. Just because we can do something doesn't necessarily mean we should do it.

I've come to understand that downtime can provide an opportunity to reconnect with our spirituality. It's a chance to rediscover the person we were always meant to be, preparing ourselves for a brighter future.

Utilize this time effectively; it can significantly benefit your overall well-being. Instead of complaining during a slow season, seize the opportunity to position yourself for success. Enhance your skills by enrolling in courses, reading books, or pursuing internships to aid in your personal growth. Remember that growth is possible even when circumstances aren't ideal. Just like trees, we can thrive where we are planted.

As a Christian, I find the life of the Apostle Paul to be a powerful example of God's ability to transform individuals through grace. Paul, who was once strongly opposed to Christianity, left behind valuable teachings on how to live as a Christian. Despite being imprisoned, he wrote multiple books in the Bible that continue to have a significant impact on people's lives today.

Always be mindful of the message to ensure clear communication. Remember that your personal development can significantly influence who and what you choose to listen to. Continuously strive to improve yourself by setting and working toward goals. It's important to remember that reaching your destination takes time, but you can adjust your strategy anytime.

Know that you are designed for success. Reinventing yourself is your business and your responsibility. Do what you can, where you can, with the resources available to you at the present moment. Train your mind to think ahead and plan for the future.

The lessons you're learning from your trials today will serve as your inspiration to persevere when faced with other challenges on your journey. In the end, it will all be worth it.

Have you ever felt mistreated, misunderstood, or judged? If so, the best way to seek revenge is to improve yourself. You can achieve a more peaceful, fulfilling, and healed life by pursuing self-discovery and self-forgiveness. I have chosen to become a life coach, consultant, speaker, and trainer to assist others in finding their inner light.

At times, I have embarked on endeavors that held great importance to me, but the hurdles I encountered made me question whether they were worth pursuing. Nevertheless, I recognized the need to summon my inner warrior and confront these challenges with heightened determination. I strive to become my own hero and firmly believe that I can overcome any obstacle because I am a child of God.

It's crucial to find specific moments for introspection, to ponder impactful questions, and to confront our deepest apprehensions. By doing so, we can gain valuable insights about ourselves, our values, and our aspirations, enabling us to make informed decisions and lead a more fulfilling life.

Once we understand how to stand our ground fearlessly, we can follow our hearts, live in joy, and address our insecurities. If we want to transform our lives, it is our responsibility to unlearn certain things, eliminate toxic behaviors, and break free from the constraints that hinder our growth.

As I continue to mature, I understand that life has an expiration date. Therefore, I must keep showing up in style, enjoying the journey, and holding onto the vision. I have stopped saving the good stuff for special occasions and now fully embrace the present moment.

We live in a time where, as women, we must actively pursue and develop our strengths to better prepare ourselves for the challenges that come our way. Through this journey, we become more knowledgeable, adaptable, and joyful. It is also a time to be more mindful of our spiritual, mental, physical, financial, and even social well-being. This encompasses the overall satisfaction of our lives. Let's be intentional about making a difference, starting with ourselves.

In the realm of self-improvement, presenting ourselves well is of great importance. Life is a continuous voyage of discovery, and traveling provides another avenue for learning about ourselves and others. Embracing and appreciating different cultures offers an opportunity to expand our knowledge and understanding, as well as learn their values. I believe it's also wonderful to know and respect these values. When I traveled to Nigeria for a trade mission trip in 2017, a trip I had always dreamed of taking with my children to visit the motherland, my eyes were opened to many new experiences and perspectives.

Dr. Erhabor Ighodaro and his wife, the former vice mayor of the City of Miami Gardens, led this mission, which took us to two different places: Abuja, the capital of Nigeria, and Benin City.

While competition is a common element of American culture, my experience in Nigeria was vastly different. I learned so much from my African sisters. I was pleasantly surprised to witness a strong sense of camaraderie and support among the women there. As a woman, I felt genuinely welcomed, which instilled in me a newfound confidence. That trip also broadened my horizons regarding fashion, culture, and the transformative power of accessories. Additionally, I observed that the women in Nigeria often embraced bold colors and designs in their attire.

During our trip to Nigeria, we observed that the locals had a profound love for music and dance. They warmly welcomed us and celebrated with great joy wherever we went.

Embarking on the hero's journey involves making necessary adjustments as we encounter various experiences and challenges. Identifying our purpose and seeking guidance from a higher power can help us navigate life with more assurance, knowing that better days are ahead. It's important to manage our internal dialogue because our biggest obstacles can be the source of limiting beliefs, doubts, and fears. As individuals, we are often evaluated based on our actions and accomplishments. Fortunately, we can transform aspects of our lives that we find unfavorable. While our aspirations and objectives may vary, most people share a desire for achievement, contentment, and joy. Regardless of what these concepts signify, attaining them requires effort and dedication.

There are times when you have to make an executive decision to choose what's best for you in the present moment, which will bring you a better perspective in the future. Achieving progress requires commitment and action, as it is a process. To reach your full potential, step out of your comfort zone, determine your path, and work towards becoming the person you are meant to be.

Embracing My Flaws

It's important to embrace your flaws, uniqueness, and imperfections because they make you exceptional and beautiful. Sometimes, we need to let go of things that hold us back and dare to move forward to a new chapter in life. Remember that it's acceptable to look different from others. I used to feel self-conscious about my feet because they're a size ten since I was twelve years old, and I was bullied for it in school. However, I realized I should be grateful for having feet when I saw the people who lost their limbs in the 2010 earthquake in Haiti. Accepting and loving yourself and embracing your flaws are good ways of showing gratitude to God for the gift of life.

We have to be thankful for what we have. We need to train ourselves to live forward rather than looking back and dwelling on the things that have hurt us or did not work in the past. Let's not wait for things to be perfect to start enjoying our lives. It can be hard when you're going through a difficult time, but it's worth remembering that there are people out there who would love to be in your shoes. Seeking help can give you the tools and resources to create a brighter future and a more fulfilling life. Remember, you're not alone, and there is always hope.

I aspire to inspire hope through my life's story, leaving behind a legacy of hope. To accomplish these ambitious objectives, I strive to better myself every day, enabling me to assist in bringing them to fruition. I also understand that I must honor some standards as a child of God.

I am driven to help people achieve their fullest potential and lead by example. Investing in ourselves and taking the time to reassess, regroup, and realign our plans is important.

Improving ourselves doesn't require perfection; it just takes a willingness to start. Progress takes time, and investing in ourselves is integral to personal growth. By committing to daily self-improvement, we learn to keep pushing and hold ourselves accountable. It's important to keep making changes and learning but also to recognize that some things are beyond our control.

If you want to invest in yourself:

1. Start by setting clear objectives and taking risks.
2. Try to read self-help books, travel, or network with others.
3. Approach these experiences with grace and humility, and remember to enjoy your freedom along the way.

Life is short, so make the most of it by constantly striving to be the best version of yourself.

Make sure to express gratitude before circumstances change. It's crucial to keep moving forward, even when the path to your desired outcome is unclear. Every moment is valuable, and pursuing your passions, fulfilling your purpose, and spreading love are essential. Have you taken the time to consider what is truly important to you? It's vital to shift your perspective and take charge of your life. Each moment is unique and contributes to your journey. Time is precious, so make the most of every day. Embrace life, seek happiness, and make a positive impact on the world.

I've learned that adaptability is the key to staying on top of things. It took some time, but I now recognize the immense value of investing in my personal growth and consistently striving to improve myself.

Learning how to prioritize our mental and spiritual well-being is crucial. I know that overcoming difficult emotions can be challenging at times, but building our mental strength is a great way to do it. As leaders and entrepreneurs, it's also important to focus on our growth and development. This way, we can ensure that our actions align with our goals and values. Of course, there might be some overlap between different areas of our lives, but with a bit of clarification and prioritization, we can stay on track and keep moving forward.

Starting something new can indeed feel intimidating, but the rewards are well worth it. Investing in yourself doesn't have to be expensive or overly time-consuming, so don't allow that to deter you. Stepping out of our comfort zones and embracing change can be quite challenging.

However, taking a bold approach and having faith in yourself is a valuable investment. Doing so will prevent any regrets when you reflect on your life. Aim to consistently give your best effort and make every moment meaningful.

Mental Health and Wellness

Our emotions hold just as much importance as our physical needs since they profoundly impact our experiences and life choices. We can identify these emotions through feelings like sadness, frustration, or happiness. Fortunately, mental health experts and researchers have equipped us with self-help techniques to enhance our mental well-being, happiness, and resilience. Among these techniques, we now recognize the significance of taking adequate rest and leisure time, cultivating self-compassion, and providing ourselves with necessary support when facing challenges. To attain inner peace, we must exert control over our thoughts. Self-control is a source of power, and composed individuals can govern both themselves and others. Taking responsibility for our actions is essential to avoid relying on others to navigate life's uncertainties. Through reflection, we can learn and grow, identifying what no longer serves us. Lastly, nature serves as a valuable teacher from which we can glean important lessons.

In 2020, many of us had to tap into our inner strength to navigate the challenges posed by the pandemic. The restrictions on in-person interactions presented difficulties for some, but they also encouraged the exploration of alternative means of connecting and engaging in more meaningful conversations, even from a distance. This period also provided an opportunity for rest, rejuvenation, and self-discovery. Establishing healthy boundaries becomes crucial for safeguarding our energy and upholding our values.

By thinking differently, you can achieve different outcomes and exhibit other behaviors. It's important to train yourself to stay motivated uniquely because you never know who may be inspired by your actions.

Romans 12:18 (NIV) says, "If it is possible, as far as it depends on you, live at peace with everyone."

No matter who we are, as long as we are alive, we go through different phases and experience a series of victories and defeats. In 2021, two female athletes, Naomi Osaka and Simone Biles, garnered attention for openly discussing their mental health. Alongside their remarkable athletic abilities, they emphasized the importance of prioritizing mental wellness. Their courage will inspire young people facing similar challenges to seek help and reduce the stigma surrounding mental health issues.

Developing critical thinking skills to enhance our cognitive abilities is crucial. A calm state of mind is a valuable asset that can help us navigate the constantly changing world more easily. Maintaining inner peace is vital because everything evolves over time, so let's learn to be more adaptable and enjoy the process.

During challenging moments when we yearn for inner peace, it's essential to be attentive to the direction of our thoughts. A constructive step toward this goal would be to establish an "emotional bank account." Since we all experience a range of emotions, it's vital to maintain a positive balance that will enable us to accumulate emotional reserves over time.

Taking care of your mental health is essential for your overall well-being. You can achieve this by being mindful of the sounds you expose yourself to and interpreting messages in a healthy way. It's important not to set unrealistic expectations to prevent disappointment. Striving for balance in all areas of life is crucial, as an excess of anything can be harmful.

Improving your overall well-being is within reach! Simply try some breathing techniques. Experiment with mindfulness and take a silent walk. The key is to find what brings you joy. And when you're feeling down, music can be a real game-changer. Additionally, discovering your rhythm while exercising can be incredibly empowering! Starting each day with prayer and gratitude is an effective way to maintain excellent mental health.

When managing your time and energy, it's important to be selective about what you consume. I recommend seeking out motivational speeches, church sermons, or uplifting gospel music. I have found Joel Osteen's teachings to be particularly inspiring and have incorporated some of his insights into my work. Joyce Meyer's messages are also worth considering, as they offer a nurturing sense of guidance akin to that of a trusted mother figure and have reminded me of the invaluable wisdom my mother imparted. Other notable speakers to check out include Dr. Myles Monroe, TD Jakes, and Priscilla Shirer.

Finding motivation can be facilitated by using social media as a helpful tool. If you are uncertain about how to begin, you may consider searching for "motivational speeches" on YouTube. With an overload of results available, we recommend that you take your time to identify the one that resonates with you the most.

Philippians 4:6-7 (NIV) says, "Do not be anxious about anything, but in every situation, by prayer and petition, with thanksgiving, present your requests to God. And the peace of God, which transcends all understanding, will guard your hearts and your minds in Christ Jesus."

Seek to improve your mood when you're dealing with moments of despair. Several things can help, such as finding reasons to be grateful, reading God's word, praying, listening to uplifting songs or tunes, and even humming or whistling, which can make you feel better. Just be mindful of avoiding songs that may trigger negative emotions. If you find yourself slipping into a negative spiral, make a conscious effort to pull yourself out as quickly as possible.

Throughout the years, I've attended various classes to gain skills that assist me in handling life's challenges. One particular course that I participated in was called "Art of Living." During this program, I learned breathing techniques and the significance of silence. The exercises taught were either calming or energizing, depending on their purpose. I also learned some exercises for practicing mindfulness. The instructors suggested that sometimes it is good to stay quiet since silence can be a powerful form of communication. Classes like this can be found everywhere these days.

Finally, it's crucial to acknowledge that prioritizing your own well-being is not selfish. It's imperative to distance yourself from toxic relationships that can drain and damage you. Choose to surround yourself with individuals who motivate and empower you.

Spiritual Health

As I've progressed through life, I've gained a better understanding of the various stages of my personal and spiritual journey. It has become clear to me that holding onto the past and expecting things to remain constant is not a practical approach, as the world is in a constant state of evolution.

My relationship with God has always been a source of strength and comfort, especially during the most challenging times in my life. I highly recommend nurturing your own relationship with God by making it an ongoing, two-way communication. Instead of merely praying for your needs, try praying about everything and consider God as a supportive companion and guide. Learn to appreciate the miracles and beauty around you as God works in His own way. Commit comforting verses from the Bible to memory. This practice can significantly benefit your spiritual well-being.

It's essential to stay true to your personal beliefs and values, even when cultural practices may challenge them. Always prioritize your values and nurture them above all else.

Understand that spirituality may have different meanings for each individual. It can have a positive impact on the decisions we make. Be selective about the spiritual leaders you choose to follow, and remember that spirituality is not the same as religion. While religion has a structure, spirituality is more personal.

Recognize the gifts bestowed upon you by God and nurture them. Acknowledge that these gifts are divine blessings, and it is your responsibility to utilize them in a manner that brings pride to Him. Cultivate a profound belief in a higher power and elevate your spiritual awareness.

1 Peter 4:10 (NIV) says, "As each one has received a special gift, employ it in serving one another as good stewards of the manifold grace of God."

Repositioning/ Self-Realization

Acknowledging and appreciating constructive feedback is a crucial component of personal growth. By remaining mindful of our actions and actively seeking to learn from our mistakes, we can significantly improve the overall quality of our lives. Personally, I've experienced substantial benefits from engaging in developmental training programs that have aided me in enhancing my communication skills and emotional management. These acquired skills have empowered me to forge stronger connections with others in various roles, including as an individual, parent, sibling, and friend.

To become a better leader:

1. Focus on communication and emotional intelligence.

2. Take targeted training programs and reflect on your progress regularly to make necessary adjustments.

3. Learn to talk about life challenges, happiness, joy, health, and prosperity for ourselves and others.

As an Entrepreneur

As an entrepreneur, recognizing the importance of investing in yourself is just as vital as investing in your business. Taking necessary breaks is essential, as it ranks among the best actions you can take for your well-being. Identifying your limitations and achieving a balanced life is critical, akin to what I refer to as personal risk management.

It's imperative to remember to care for ourselves while diligently pursuing our goals. It's all too easy to fall into the trap of pushing ourselves relentlessly, but in the end, such an approach isn't sustainable. Prioritizing both our physical and mental health is fundamental to achieving our desired outcomes. Always remain attuned to your body's signals and take breaks when necessary.

Furthermore, it's essential to acquire financial management skills to effectively care for both your business and household.

In the business realm, the allure of resorting to dishonest practices can be strong. However, it is of utmost importance to uphold honesty and integrity, taking full responsibility for our actions.

The ability to discern between personal and non-personal matters is a crucial skill that entrepreneurs must cultivate. This skill equips them to make well-informed decisions and sound investments, ultimately contributing to their overall success.

Unconventional Investments

Set the tone for the day with a positive and grateful prayer. Instead of worrying about impressing others, focus on personal growth and set challenging goals to work towards. Building wisdom and strength through the acquisition of knowledge is a powerful tool, and one should never underestimate its importance. This can be achieved through reading books, listening to podcasts, and attending training. Self-talk can also be a helpful tool to stay motivated. Practicing deep breathing techniques and approaching life with a positive outlook are recommended. Sometimes, unconventional choices based on personal experience and knowledge may become necessary.

Create a list of things that would enhance your life, such as places to visit or live. Write about what success means to you, the type of relationships you want to have, and more. However, avoid becoming obsessed with it. Make adjustments as you grow and mature, as your dreams and desires can change, and you can make wiser decisions. We are constantly evolving, and change is inevitable.

Always strive for peace, regardless of what is happening in your life or your surroundings. It's essential to change any habits that aren't benefiting you, take time to pray, and maintain a calm heart. Remember to avoid getting too caught up in winning and instead focus on learning from every experience. Please pay attention to the small things and appreciate them.

Age is not the determining factor of maturity and enlightenment; it is based on your comprehension of life and the world. Allow yourself to be receptive to the light that emanates from within. Take the opportunity to reflect inwardly and connect with the guidance and wisdom bestowed upon you by your creator.

It's understandable to sometimes doubt yourself and your capabilities. On the other hand, it's essential to recognize your strengths and the positive impact you can have on your life, family, and community. You deserve to believe in yourself and your abilities and not limit your own success. Let's work together to overcome self-sabotage and focus on achieving your goals and values.

Maintaining an active lifestyle to avoid boredom is important for our well-being. Finding a balance between your energy levels and appreciating life's joys is crucial. Don't let fear limit your potential; strive to align your ambition with your capabilities. Investing in yourself means being open to learning in various ways. Children and seniors offer valuable insights and knowledge. Children live in the present and lead uncomplicated lives. Seniors possess abundant experience and wisdom, especially concerning what truly matters.

Observing young children is a delight because of their boundless energy and unbridled joy. I admire the fearlessness and optimism of children as they face each day with a clean slate, unburdened by past grievances. They exude confidence and find pleasure in the simplest things. As adults, we can learn from their example and infuse more clarity and happiness into our lives. Let's adopt their creativity, courage, and zest for life to experience adulthood more intensely.

Children excel at finding joy and excitement. They have a knack for making things enjoyable and always prioritize pleasure. They possess a captivating and contagious joy that permeates everything they do. They revel in the thrill of adventure, eagerly exploring and discovering the world around them. Fearlessly pursuing new friendships, they thrive on hands-on experiences that allow them to learn and grow. Undoubtedly, actions are the most effective way to impart knowledge to them.

As we grow older, we develop unique qualities that make us special. I've observed that seniors have a wealth of life experience from which we can benefit when we take the time to listen to them. They also tend to be very humble and avoid any behavior that might be seen as competitive or arrogant.

Listening to our elders can be incredibly valuable. My mother once told me, 'You can never live long enough to know everything firsthand.' Listening to the experiences and perspectives of others can teach us so much and help us make necessary changes to improve ourselves.

The older generation possesses a wealth of knowledge from their life experiences. They believe that money isn't the answer to everything and emphasize the importance of self-care. They also suggest not worrying about things beyond our control and taking things one step at a time.

Take the time to learn from the people around you. Listen to your elders and observe your children. Cherish your moments with them; they can enrich your life and help you understand what truly matters.

Identifying and pursuing the right resources and opportunities is crucial for achieving our objectives. By being adaptable to change and taking responsibility for our lives, we can overcome any fears we may have about being on our own.

It may seem counterintuitive, but failures, mistakes, and bad decisions can provide valuable lessons that guide us toward the right path. Numerous successful individuals have gained wisdom from their mistakes, and this knowledge can propel us forward, helping us overcome obstacles and achieve our goals.

The path of our transformation is shaped by the choices we make and how we handle the situations that come our way, along with our intentions and level of awareness. It takes courage to break away from patterns that hinder personal growth. Remember that you can explore different avenues. Just know that we are all here to achieve great things during our time on this earth.

Reader Reflection

"There is a time for everything, and a season for every activity under the heavens: a time to be born and a time to die, a time to plant and a time to uproot."
- Ecclesiastes 3:1-2 (NIV)

"Rejoice in the Lord always; again, I will say, Rejoice. Let your reasonableness be known to everyone. The Lord is at hand; do not be anxious about anything, but in everything by prayer and supplication with thanksgiving let your requests be made known to God. And the peace of God, which surpasses all understanding, will guard your hearts and your minds in Christ Jesus."
- Philippians 4:4-7 (NIV)

"But the fruit of the Spirit is love, joy, peace, patience, kindness, goodness, faithfulness, gentleness, self-control; against such things there is no law."
- Galatians 5:22-23 (NIV)

"Put on the whole armor of God, that you may be able to stand against the schemes of the devil."
- Ephesians 6:11 (NIV)

Seek peace and avoid loud and aggressive people because they can irritate your spirit.

If you compare yourself with others, you may become vain and bitter.

Enjoy your achievements as well as the preparation that you are doing now for a better tomorrow.

Journal Prompts

In our life, we are both the judge and jury. We have the opportunity to live the best life. We are responsible for the choices that we make, both short-term and long-term.

1. What are your dreams, desires, and visions?

2. What are your main goals in life?

3. How do you invest in yourself?

4. How do you need to invest in yourself to reach your goals?

5. Are you making decisions that will lead you to the path of your promised land?

Tips to Adjust the Volume

- Treat yourself like a special person.

- Relax, renew, recharge.

- Focus on today.

- Learn to let go.

- Make the most of every opportunity.

- Give your confidence a boost.

- Enjoy life with simple joy.

- Practice acceptance.

CHAPTER ELEVEN
Lessons I Learned from Talina

How we make choices, and the people we allow into our lives really matter. Talina, my mom, became my best friend, mentor, and confidant over time. As a teenager, my relationship with my mom was challenging. However, I came to understand that her strictness was her way of shaping me into a better person. Although my mom is no longer with me, the values she taught me still resonate with me. The most significant lesson she imparted to me was to love God and appreciate the blessings in my life. She taught me not to focus so much on what I don't have but on what I am going to do to get it. She never demanded perfection from me and didn't believe in comparing herself to others or relying on luck. Instead, she believed in grace, miracles, hard work, determination, confidence, and charisma. Above all, she always stressed the importance of living a life of integrity.

She believed that life is all about growth. Part of growth is that some experiences can be personal but not limited to our own. We can also learn from the mistakes and successes of others because our time is limited.

At 79, my mother once told me, "People often say that life is short, but it can also be very long. Just look at me about to turn 80." She reflected on how, when she was 40, my mother never thought she would reach this age. She believed that it's essential to make both short-term and long-term plans and to have faith that you'll live a long life. No matter how young you are now, you can achieve great things.

Your age should not define who you are, whether you are young or old. Don't allow anyone to look down on you because of your age. Instead, set an example for others in the way you express yourself, conduct yourself, show love, have faith, and maintain purity.

Talina possessed the qualities of a strong, confident leader. She was strategic in choosing her battles and resilient in bouncing back. Through life's lessons, I have learned to value what I have in the present moment. Reflecting on my past, I am grateful for my mother's priceless advice.

Taking breaks and re-energizing yourself is crucial, especially during tough times. Don't let the challenges you're facing today take root, and don't allow discouragements and disappointments to make you settle for less. Eventually, these things will be behind you, and you'll realize that these hard times were lessons to strengthen your faith and develop your character. Instead, shift your mindset and confidently believe that things will get better because they will. Remember, material possessions aren't the most valuable things in life.

When I used to visit my mom in Haiti, our conversations about faith were always meaningful. She instilled in me the belief that I am a child of God and can accomplish anything with His help. Her guidance and encouragement continue to inspire me today, even though I miss her dearly.

Being aware of our words is crucial, as they carry much weight. Speaking from a place of negative emotions like anger, envy, jealousy, or hate can have long-lasting effects. Once words are said, they cannot be unsaid; that's why we should be deliberate when we speak. I used to question my mother's habit of repeating herself when giving advice but later understood that it was because she cared about me and wanted me to listen. As a result, I now adopt the same approach with my children occasionally.

I understand the situation better now, but I would like to have a conversation with her for further clarification. Nevertheless, I can now act on the knowledge I have gained. I want to share a piece of advice she always gave me: "Get started and make adjustments along the way."

It's important to learn to value what you currently have so you won't regret it when it's gone. My mother was an extraordinary person who lived until she was 85. She was an entrepreneur, survivor, counselor, philosopher, and wore many other hats, as evidenced during her funeral. I learned more stories about how she had impacted people's lives through her advice. She was my role model, and her guidance helped me through difficult times. Her bravery and determination continue to inspire me greatly.

My mom passed down her contagious laughter to me. It had the power to bring joy to anyone's day, including mine. Even in times of pain, she could mask it with her laughter.

Talina accomplished much in her life despite her educational limitations. During my third-grade studies, my mother would request that I recite the lesson material to her, only to later find out that she had never read the material herself, but she knew that I was not ready.

Despite her limited reading and writing skills, she remarkably understood the importance of education, family, economics, and generosity. Her insights were priceless and greatly appreciated.

Yes, my mother was an extraordinary woman; she possessed a wise perspective on life. She always encouraged me to take a moment to focus on the promises of God and the wonderful things in life. Despite being a strong woman, she was an incredibly caring individual. She had a habit of waking up early to enjoy her coffee alone, which was her favorite time to connect with God and plan for the day ahead.

I found it interesting that my mom had only worked for her mom and no one else. She had been a businesswoman since the age of 10, when she began assisting her mom in her business.

My mom believed in family, helping others grow, and economic development as the way to empower people and leave a lasting legacy. She was a true inspiration, not just for my sisters and me but for many others. Knowing that I could always count on her for advice was priceless.

In a conversation with my mother, I asked her what drove her successful business ventures. She confidently shared that success is about accumulating wealth and utilizing our skills to help ourselves and others. While education is valuable, she stressed that persistence is the key to success.

The Greatest Example

A handbook on motherhood can certainly help you become better parents, but every child and situation is unique. Fortunately, I had an amazing role model in my mother, who taught me so much about parenting by setting a great example.

Being my mom's youngest child made me stronger and more independent. My mother instilled in me the values of self-sufficiency and maturity at a young age. She taught me how to manage my affairs and care for myself. Her fear of leaving me behind only fueled my determination to be resilient.

As I matured and gained a deeper insight into life, my relationship with my mother changed. I allowed myself to become closer to her once again, and at the age of 31, I decided to get to know her as both a woman and a friend. I traveled to Haiti to spend time with her, and during that trip, she confided in me about many personal experiences and secrets that revealed her true character. This was a powerful revelation for me as a young woman because I realized that my mother was a true hero who had overcome many obstacles that were meant to break her. She also served as a valuable mentor to me.

Children observe their parents' actions as they search for their own identity. Setting a positive example and being a strong role model for the young individuals in our lives is crucial.

My mom always told me that true self-confidence is about being comfortable in your own skin without the need to compete with others. She also believed that speaking poorly about a current or former partner is unhelpful and instead recommended using past experiences to improve future relationships. She considered this the first step towards healing and moving forward. Ultimately, starting fresh and looking ahead can be the key to getting unstuck.

It's important to prioritize your well-being in a relationship. Feel free to leave if you've prayed and done everything you can but still see no improvement. Don't sacrifice your own happiness to avoid judgment from others. Instead, focus on the positive aspects of your life and plan your next steps. In today's world of division, hatred, and fear, we must be mindful of who we allow into our lives and how we handle our emotions.

My mother often said, "Mete Fanm sou ou pou'w kapab regle zafè'w tande," which means "Be strong so you can handle your own issues." She had a keen perception of my emotions, even when I tried to hide them with a smile or silence.

My mother's wise advice instilled in me a sense of practicality and a deep understanding of progress, longevity, and sustainability. Her guidance inspired me to become a coach, as she often posed thought-provoking questions that helped me discover solutions to any situation. Whenever I encountered obstacles, I would turn to my mother for support, and she would assist me without imposing her own ideas. She reminded me that challenges are only temporary and encouraged me to take a deep breath and remember my strengths. Furthermore, she instilled in me the belief that the future holds even better opportunities than the past.

In challenging times, remember that things can improve. Try to let go of resentment and seek forgiveness for yourself and others. However, be mindful of those who may take advantage of you. By being aware of your energy and resources, you can continue to make a positive impact. I've personally learned this valuable lesson in my personal growth.

In March 2019, the Global Trade Chamber of Commerce recognized me as one of the 100 most influential women in business. This was a significant honor, and I dedicated it to my mom and grandmother for paving the way for me and my family.

I am proud to be a female entrepreneur and acknowledge the hard work of the women who paved the way for me. Although my grandmother passed before my time, her values of integrity and morality have been instilled in me and other women. We must continue this legacy and strive for success.

Leaving a Legacy

Investing in yourself for a better tomorrow is the greatest legacy you can leave to humanity. Let's work together to make the world a better place. Focus your prayers on self-improvement and discovering God's purpose for your life. It's okay to accept that not all of your dreams may come true directly, but you can still plant seeds of kindness through your actions and behavior. Remember that these seeds will continue to bear fruit even after you are gone.

I often stress to my audience the importance of breaking the cycle of poverty. By making a modest monthly payment, they can acquire a life insurance policy that will have a long-term impact on their family's legacy and financial security. When we pass away, our family will be grateful for the legacy we leave behind and can enjoy the fruits of our labor.

It's heart-wrenching to witness the devastating effects of losing one's home in the community, facing foreclosure, or having to relocate due to family illness or loss. Many people need to be made aware of the resources available to them, which only adds to the difficulties of the situation. However, with proper preparation and planning, we can leverage these resources and focus on what truly matters: providing for our families. As a licensed real estate agent, investing in real estate can offer a valuable opportunity to accumulate wealth.

We can begin breaking the cycle of poverty by concentrating on our own families. As I often emphasize at the end of my radio shows, "envesti nan tèt ou pou yon demen miyò" English: "invest in yourself for a better future."

Have you used your voice today? It's the most ancient means of communication that even King Solomon himself implored to gain wisdom from God. I have chosen to leverage my voice to connect with people and instill hope through my radio show, the Koze Fanm show. Initially, I was uncertain about whether it would take off, but after being on the air for about two decades, we are still going strong. Our listeners continue to return and recommend the show to others, and our sponsors and partners have unwavering faith in the power of bringing hope to our audience through the airwaves. With the assistance of technology and social media, the potential for impact is limitless.

After almost twenty years on the air, we have expanded to various platforms and networks, including radio, TV, podcasts, magazines, websites, training, group coaching, speaking engagements, and now this book. Our goal is to spread positivity and inspire others to make a difference. We should strive to reach our highest potential and motivate others to do the same. Let's continue to plant seeds of greatness wherever we go.

It is of utmost importance to me that my children and anyone I encounter always maintain self-respect and recognize the greatness within them. I consistently remind my daughter of her uniqueness and beauty, and I encourage both of my children to avoid comparing themselves to others. Above all, I want them to understand that they possess the capability and potential to create a fulfilling and prosperous life.

Exuding excellence is crucial to me as a Christian woman, as I strive to maintain the highest level of integrity and uphold a legacy of faithfulness. When you are a child of God, certain standards must be honored because He has always kept His promises, and I aim to reflect that same level of commitment in all aspects of my life.

I am fully aware that what I do today will shape my legacy. Therefore, I am determined to put in the necessary effort and intelligence to make a positive impact. I aspire to be recognized for the positive changes I bring about and my ability to inspire others. Ultimately, I want to motivate and empower others while I am still here.

I trust that you have recognized the boundless possibilities ahead of you. You will be the driving force for transformation and establish an everlasting mark of distinction. Let us work together in unison to adjust the settings and focus on our strengths until our communication resonates with unwavering clarity.

Reader Reflection

"Blessed is the one who does not walk in step with the wicked or stand in the way that sinners take or sit in the company of mockers, but whose delight is in the law of the LORD, and who meditates on his law day and night. That person is like a tree planted by streams of water, which yields its fruit in season and whose leaf does not wither— whatever they do prospers." - Psalms 1:1-3 (NIV)

Journal Prompts:

You are capable, compassionate, and intelligent individuals with the potential to create a rewarding and prosperous life.

1. What action can you take to be the change you want to see?

2. What legacy will you leave?

3. How would life look if you focused less on what others might think or how things might turn out?

Tips to Adjust the Volume:

*   Charity begins at home.

*   Give your children a voice.

*   Inspire confidence with your presence.

*   Share how past generations overcame adversity.

*   Have an open discussion about goals and values.

*   Don't take everything to heart.

*   Apply knowledge and understanding.

Use your power in a more productive way. Remove yourself from situations that don't contribute to your happiness, such as disrespect, verbal, emotional, or physical abuse.

It's okay to live a joyful, prosperous life. Don't let anybody tell you that protecting your peace of mind and happiness is selfish or that you are better than others. It's simply that happy people tend to be more productive. This has helped me become a leader for others in my life. Coaching training has also improved my relationships with my children, sisters, and others.

Although my mother was the guiding star in my life, there are a few major lessons I remember learning from my father. He always told me that I am called to be a leader, and as a leader, I must work to protect my reputation at all costs. He also taught me to be careful about whom I choose as friends because those we hang out with tend to influence our character.

As a child of God, it does matter who we spend time with. My father used to share a French proverb that goes, "Dis-moi qui tu fréquentes, et je te dirai qui tu es," which translates to "Tell me who you hang out with, and I'll tell you who you are." This applies when assessing people's character. Be mindful of who you spend time with, listen to, watch, or read.

One of the most significant lessons he taught me was to always be cautious because someone is always watching when you least expect it. He shared this wisdom with me when I was just 15, many years before the era of social media, and it has always stayed with me.

A couple of years later, at the age of 17, my mom and I were not getting along very well. My mom called my father to intervene. He had a conversation with me, reminding me to be discerning about the company I kept and who I allowed into my life.

The concept of leadership was instilled in me by my father. When I expressed to him that I was still quite young, he replied that leadership is not determined by age but can be learned. He emphasized that our values shape our decisions. Inspired by his guidance, I eagerly delved into learning more about leadership by reading books on the subject. It became clear to me that I needed to be mindful of this aspect of my life.

Although they played very different roles in my life, both of my parents shaped me into the woman I have become. I've noticed young girls referring to themselves as 'queens.' Everyone has their own way of doing and seeing things. However, in my perspective, it takes training to learn self-control and build character to become a queen. These attributes are earned through life experiences, making things more achievable.

In life, we often have to prioritize what we must do before we can do what we want to do. Advancing to the next level requires evolving into a different version of yourself. It can be uncomfortable at times, but staying on course, keeping your eyes on the prize, and not avoiding the process is key.

Reader Reflection
Journal Prompts

1. How have your parents shaped your path in life?

2. In what ways are you similar to your parents? In what ways are you different?

3. What's something you've always wanted to say to your parents? Write it down in an unsent letter.

Tips to Adjust the Volume

- Transform failure into success.
- Simple acts of kindness make a world of difference.
- Keep things in perspective.
- Smile and let your positive side shine.
- Take charge of your life.
- Be a giver more than a receiver.
- Always look your best.

CHAPTER TWELVE
Shaping Your Legacy

Who am I, and who do I want to become? What will be my contribution during my time on Earth? Leaving a lasting impact involves finding a way to serve others, learning from our experiences, and using our wisdom to guide our actions. Learning to position ourselves to recognize God's providence is crucial.

We should acknowledge our mistakes and celebrate our successes while helping others with our knowledge. We must also prioritize our self-worth, beliefs, and spirituality. By making positive choices for ourselves and our loved ones, we can make a meaningful difference in the world. Let's set new standards, strive for improvement, and refuse to let mistakes hold us back. Sharing love and positivity with those around us is essential for fostering a positive and supportive environment.

Legacy revolves around uncovering a deep-seated purpose. Progress remains elusive without taking action; it's not enough to have faith alone—it must be supported by bold moves. Find what truly motivates you and pursue it with tenacity and courage, letting your motivation overcome any obstacle you encounter.

If you had one million dollars to spare, how and where would you choose to allocate it?

A legacy is a remarkable and enduring heritage passed down from previous generations. It symbolizes a valuable entity preserved from the past, which continues to exist in the present.

Jeremiah 33:6

Behold, I will bring to it health and healing, and I will heal them; and I will reveal to them an abundance of peace and truth.

To leave a lasting legacy, it is crucial to bestow blessings upon your children. One highly effective method of nurturing their potential is to consistently shower them with praise and motivate them to create a positive impact on this generation.

Psalm 122:7

"May there be peace within your walls and security within your palaces."

One's legacy cannot be solely defined by age or years of service. Dedication to a mission that transcends our own lifetime is a delicate endeavor. Consider planting the seeds of excellence that will yield a fruitful harvest in the future.

When it comes to leaving a legacy, you have the choice to be remembered as either a helper or an enabler. Personally, I aspire to be a positive influence on those around me and aim to leave a lasting impact. I measure my legacy by the meaningful moments I share with others, my decisions, and my actions throughout my life. I have learned and grown from my mistakes and continue to do so in each phase of my life.

While there are many not-for-profit organizations, the needs are still substantial. Everyone can contribute by volunteering, donating to a foundation, or becoming a philanthropist. If the time has come for you to serve, do so with integrity, and remember that treating people with dignity is essential.

My home country, Haiti, endured two devastating earthquakes in 2010 and 2021. Despite receiving significant donations, no lasting progress was achieved. This underscores the need for sustainable changes to be implemented; otherwise, history will continue to repeat itself without meaningful improvements. It's time to shift our mindset and prioritize lasting change. We must think about the future of the young people who have lost their families.

Determining how best to support and prioritize assistance for those in need can be challenging. Therefore, finding appropriate resources to gain clarity in these situations is essential. Fortunately, there are several ways to achieve this. To better support recovery, it's crucial to identify needs and determine the appropriate aid.

A highly effective approach to addressing the issue is by providing individuals with education on how to create opportunities and increase their productivity. This empowerment enables them to take control of their lives and rebuild sustainably and enduringly. Alongside rebuilding homes, it's vital that we invest in long-term strategies to instill hope and confidence in people.

An impactful method to combat poverty in a nation is by promoting a change in perspective through education. By motivating people to explore the various possibilities for personal advancement, they can develop a positive outlook on life and unlock their full potential. Embracing a positive mindset can significantly enhance an individual's overall well-being.

Some ways to do this include:

- Helping the impoverished find ways to take action to rebuild on their own

- Equipping people with knowledge and the tools they need to strategize and figure out situations on their own

- Creating awareness and raising consciousness around the issue of poverty

- Take action to make education more accessible

- Instill confidence by reassuring and empowering people affected by poverty

Sustainable economic development relies on creating jobs through both production and education. Supporting trade schools and promoting literacy are effective ways to achieve this goal. Education boosts confidence and increases earnings, making it the logical first step toward alleviating extreme poverty.

Ensuring access to basic human necessities like food, healthcare, education, sanitation, and employment opportunities is crucial. However, it's essential to identify the root causes of the problem before providing assistance to avoid enabling dependency.

It's important to acknowledge that there's no universal remedy, but we can take action. Even small efforts can have a significant impact, so let's come together to bring about constructive changes and enhance people's well-being."

Our Legacy as Women

As we journey through life and plant the seeds of goodness for a bountiful harvest, it's crucial to remember that our choices wield significant influence. Achieving success in both business and our personal lives is most fulfilling when it is shared with others. Living with good intentions can pave the way for incredible blessings and the favor of God. As a woman, a mother, and a community advocate, the creation of a lasting legacy is of utmost importance to me. I endeavor to share my wisdom and knowledge while collaborating with others to uplift those in our midst.

Psalm 37:25 "I was young and now I am old, yet I have never seen the righteous forsaken or their children begging bread."

Staying true to your authentic self is essential for building a lasting legacy. Your actions and behaviors serve as a guiding example for future generations. It's important to make the most of each day and prioritize self-care because we cannot predict when our time will come to an end. Living each day to its fullest is paramount, and striving for inner peace by maintaining a clear conscience and fostering a positive outlook are crucial steps in this journey.

The maternal figure within a family possesses an extraordinary ability to conceal their personal struggles while displaying unwavering strength in the face of adversity, allowing them to persevere and continue pushing forward.

I have a vivid memory from when I was approximately six years old. It was a Sunday evening, and I was suffering from an asthma attack. My mother rushed me to the emergency room at the general hospital in Port-au-Prince. As the nurses conducted the triage, they asked my mom to place me on the examination room table. She later recounted to me that, while I was being examined, she looked under the table and saw the lifeless bodies of seven young children. Can you imagine the shock and horror? It was a defining moment for my mom. She gathered her strength and fervently prayed to God for a resolution to the situation.

She ultimately decided to take me back home and apply natural remedies to aid in my healing. She firmly believed that, regardless of the circumstances, God had the final say. As I grew older and became a mother myself, I understood the depth of her faith when she would say that the angels of the Lord encamp around those who fear Him, and He delivers them.

She explained to me that while she felt sorry for me being sick, her heart ached even more for the parents of those children who couldn't make it, primarily due to their lack of financial means. Often, tragedies like these occur simply because of the absence of money and resources. So, she resolved to take action. In her business, whenever a woman approached her seeking financial assistance, she would provide them with merchandise, whether it was textiles or beauty supplies, to kickstart a business venture. Some of these transactions were structured as loans, while others were gifts.

Some of these women disappeared, while others diligently grew their businesses by repaying the loans and purchasing more merchandise. Those who put in a sincere effort not only improved their own lives but also made a positive impact on their families. It's far too common for us to become ensnared in the idea of perpetuating dependency. I firmly believe that when individuals are personally invested in their progress, it not only boosts their self-esteem and dignity but also presents an opportunity for personal growth and entrepreneurship.

The lesson here is that demonstrating compassion doesn't mean simply handing out money; it means empowering individuals to multiply their resources. We need to break the cycle and create opportunities for change. My mother instilled in me the importance of encouraging people to work because it helps them preserve their dignity and self-respect. I was raised with the belief that we reside in an abundant universe and must express gratitude for and acknowledge all the riches of life. Wealth should be regarded as a state of being, not solely measured by the size of our bank accounts. Let's manifest abundance in all aspects of our lives.

I firmly believe in giving back, but I've also learned that you can't give from an empty well. To me, there are numerous ways to give back. First and foremost, we must prioritize our own well-being in order to better assist others.

As I continue to mature in life and faith, I've come to realize that my past regrets are transforming into valuable lessons. It has become increasingly clear to me that we must align our intentions towards producing tangible results, recognizing that even a journey of a thousand miles commences with a single step.

From a very young age, my mother imparted numerous lessons to me, shaping me into a responsible woman. She would often say, "Work hard while learning how to work smart," and she instilled in me the practice of beginning every endeavor with prayer.

She nurtured me into a resilient businesswoman and a faithful child of God. While these teachings may appear simple, they are part of a legacy that has been passed down through generations, from my grandmother to my mother and now to my children. The core principle of this legacy revolves around the idea that by prioritizing God in our lives, He guides us to where we are meant to be.

When my mother passed away, I took on the responsibility of preparing her obituary. While I knew a great deal about her, I sought insights from someone who had known her longer than I had – my uncle, my mother's brother. He shared that my great-grandmother had embraced

Christianity when my grandmother was just a toddler, and from that point onward, our family has held steadfast to Christian values.

Creating a lasting legacy is an endeavor rooted in belief in one's dreams and the capacity to broaden one's horizons. It involves finding balance, safeguarding one's health, nurturing inner peace, and preserving energy while continually elevating one's thinking. It entails activating faith and embracing maturity as guiding principles.

2 Timothy 1:7

7 For God has not given us the spirit of fear; but of power, and of love, and of a sound mind.

It's time to welcome new frequencies: Take charge of the thoughts you allow in as they shape the words that manifest in your life. This way, you can triumph without engaging in conflict. May you find the courage to reconsider, reassess, recalibrate, and redefine your strategies. Maintain trust in yourself, be confident, and seek knowledge, for you are on the right path to a successful journey.

As we strive to fulfill our life's purpose, fine-tuning our understanding and discovering our unique frequency is an ongoing and evolving process. Continuously redirect your focus, recharge your energy, and make necessary adjustments until your message resonates clearly. Stay optimistic because wonderful opportunities lie on the horizon.

Closing Thoughts

You possess an incredible capacity to regulate both your emotional and spiritual well-being. Achieving your dreams doesn't require you to be asleep; there are ways to turn them into reality while you're fully awake. Keep in mind that self-improvement is a gradual process, so practice patience with yourself and persist in your efforts. To preserve your inner peace, prioritize the care of your mental and physical health.

- Put God first in everything that you do. He is the maker and creator of all things.

Adjusting the volume to survive and thrive is an ongoing life practice, and cultivating the ability to make sustainable change is the outcome of this practice. There are a few ways to define the word "volume." The first is "the degree of loudness or the intensity of a sound." This is similar to the volume on your radio or any audible device. Volume can also be defined as "the amount of space occupied by a three-dimensional object, measured in cubic units (such as quarts or liters)." The concept of volume can be both tangible and intangible, so continue to make space and time to reach your greatest potential.

Some advice that may be useful:

- Development of the proper skills that we need to be more complete in our lives is vital.

- We can all learn new techniques and tricks to live a better and more fulfilling life while we are here on planet Earth.

- Growth and lessons often come from the failures and adversities of life. Just know that it's never too late to start again, and remember to be appreciative of the things that ARE working.

- Dare to be you and accept yourself unconditionally.

- If you fall, get right back up.

- Be mindful of your thoughts to better manage your feelings and self-control.

- Everything you need is within you.

- Work on developing a growth mindset.

- Know that you have the power of choice.

- Don't compare yourself to others, but surround yourself with individuals whose dreams and visions align with your own.

- Getting old is not to be feared.

- Embrace who you are becoming.

- Don't leave room for hate.

- Trouble is temporary.

- Don't depend so much on material things to be happy.

- Not everyone is going to like or understand you.

- Let go of other people's expectations.

- Do what you love.

- Let go of what no longer serves you.

- Life is beautiful. Let the sunshine in.

- Live life in full color.

- Make every moment count.

- Find stability and use your knowledge to create career growth and personal empowerment.

- Be your own biggest fan.

- There's no better time to make a difference than now.

- Increase your life satisfaction by believing in your own ability.

- Your words matter. Use them wisely.

- We should never assume that being loud is the same as being strong or that silence is a sign of weakness.

- Adjusting our frequency until the message is clear is a lifelong pursuit.

Works Cited

1. "Perinatal Depression." National Institute of Mental Health. U.S. Department of Health and Human Services. Accessed January 25, 2022. https://www.nimh.nih.gov/health/publications/perinatal-depression/index.shtml.

2. Langdon, Kimberly, ed. "Statistics on Postpartum Depression - Postpartum Depression Resources." PostpartumDepression.org, June 3, 2021. https://www.postpartumdepression.org/resources/statistics/.

Thank You:

I want to express my heartfelt gratitude to all my relatives, friends, loved ones, coaches, counselors, consultants, and everyone who contributed to bringing this book to life. Your contributions have been invaluable; this would not have been possible without your support. As you read through these pages, I am confident that you will find them both insightful and thought-provoking. Have the courage to turn your dreams into goals and the ability to turn them into actions. Keep striving for greatness, as amazing things are in store for each one of you. May God expand your horizons.

GUYLENE BERRY

www.ingramcontent.com/pod-product-compliance
Lightning Source LLC
Chambersburg PA
CBHW071327120626
46546CB00002B/468